Carole King
TAPESTRY

ISBN 978-0-634-06719-8

HAL•LEONARD® CORPORATION

7777 W. BLUEMOUND RD. P.O. BOX 13819 MILWAUKEE, WI 53213

In Australia Contact:
Hal Leonard Australia Pty. Ltd.
22 Taunton Drive   P.O. Box 5130
Cheltenham East, 3192   Victoria, Australia
Email: ausadmin@halleonard.com

Visit Hal Leonard Online at
www.halleonard.com

www.CaroleKing.com

Carole King
TAPESTRY

CONTENTS

I FEEL THE EARTH MOVE

Words and Music by
CAROLE KING

Moderate Rock

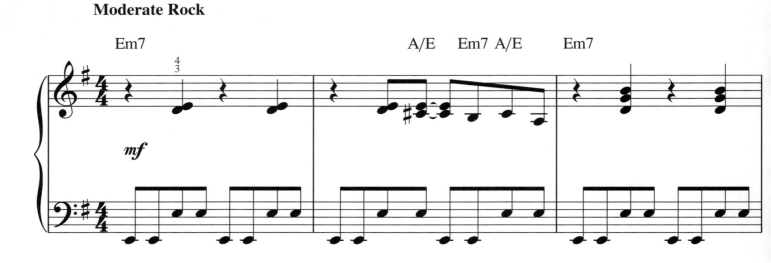

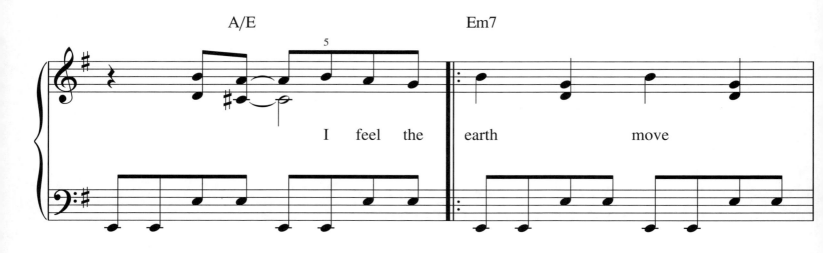

I feel the earth move

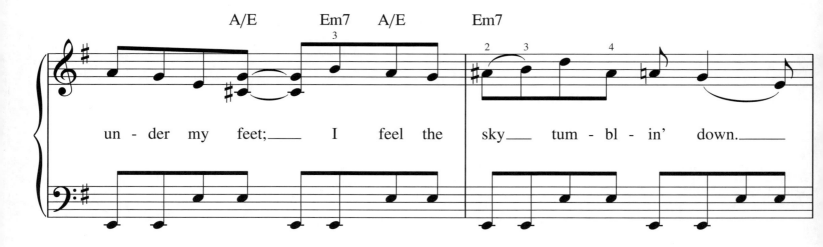

un-der my feet;___ I feel the sky___ tum-bl-in' down.___

oh,_____ dar - lin',_____ I can't stand____ it when you look

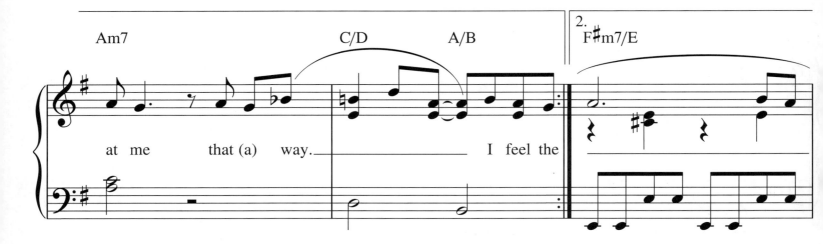

at me that (a) way._____ I feel the

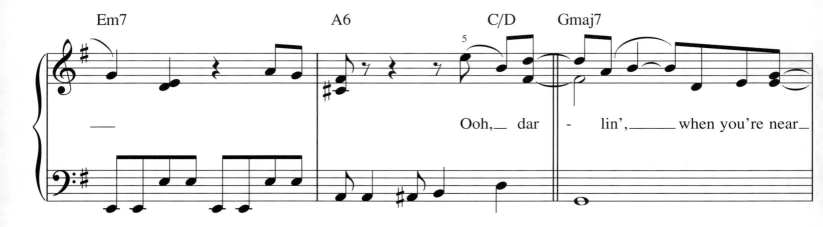

Ooh,__ dar - lin',_____ when you're near__

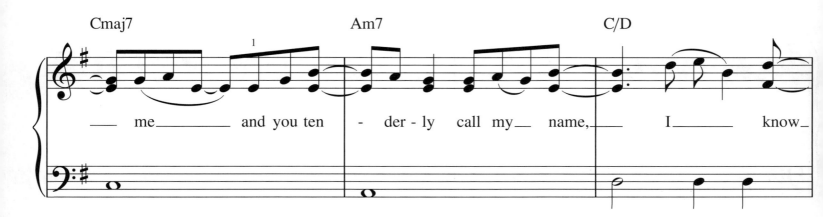

____ me_____ and you ten - der-ly call my__ name,____ I_____ know__

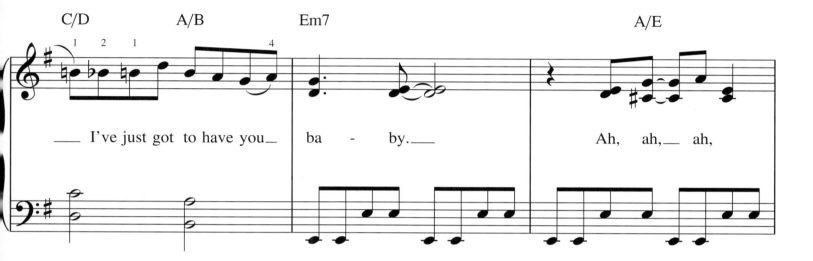

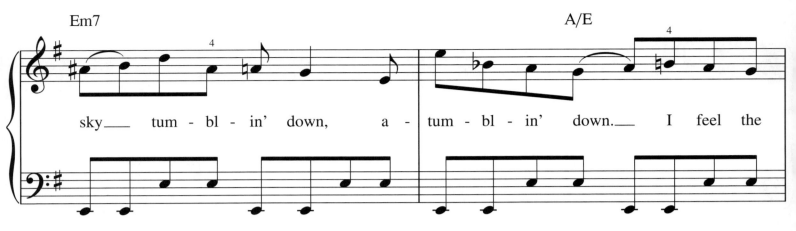

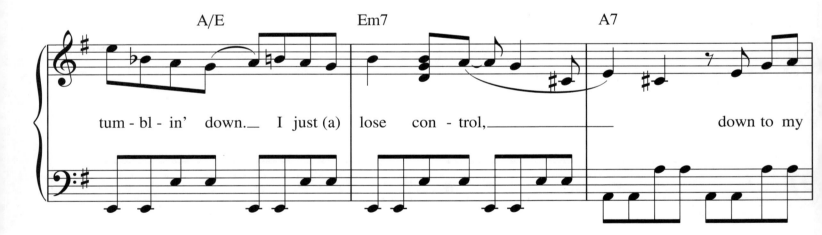

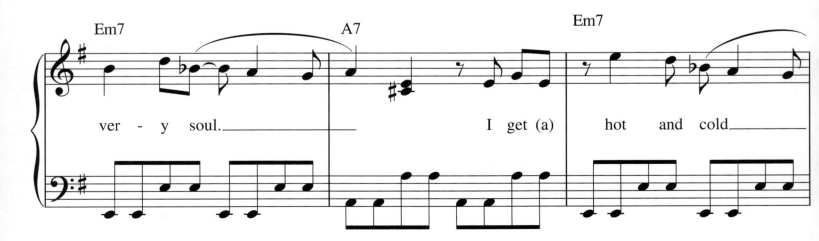

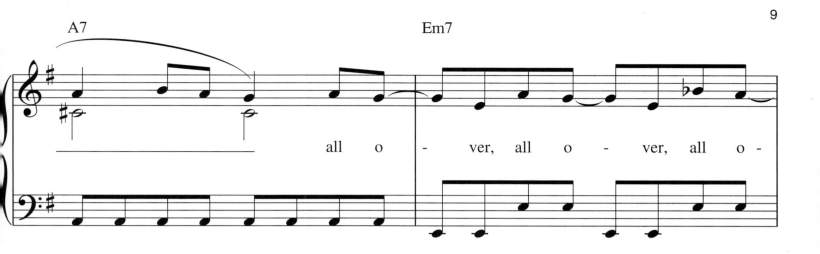

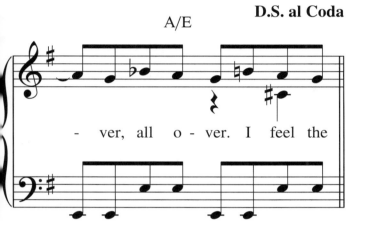

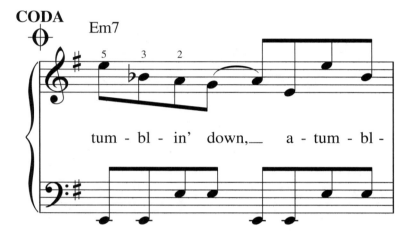

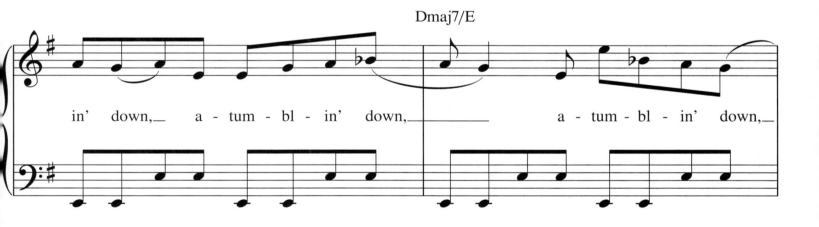

SO FAR AWAY

Words and Music by
CAROLE KING

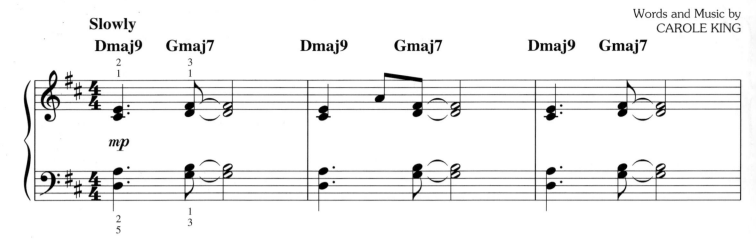

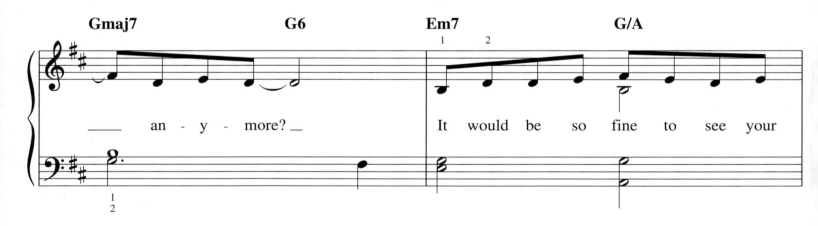

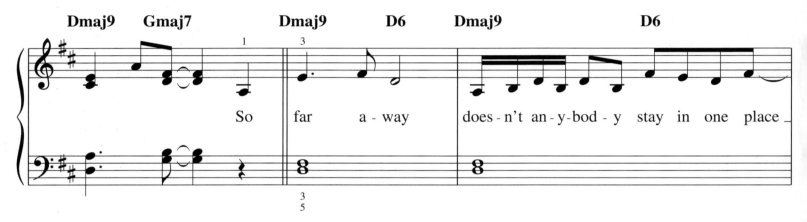

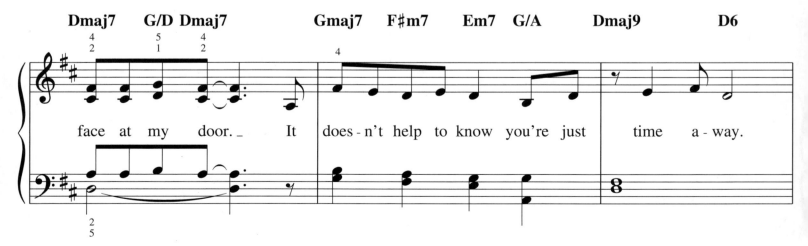

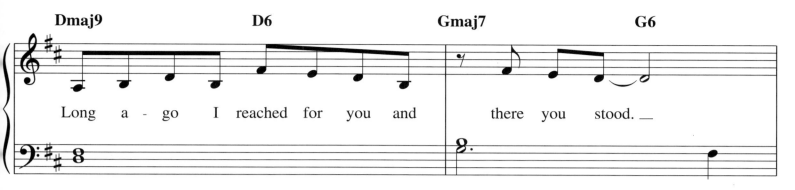

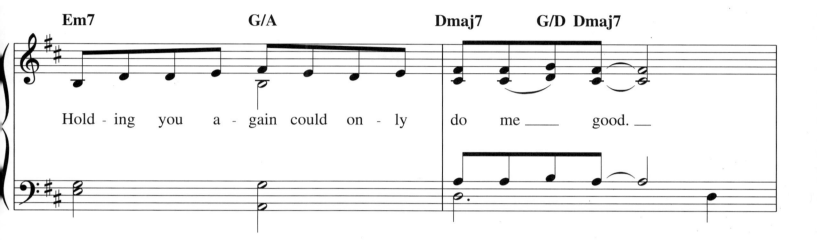

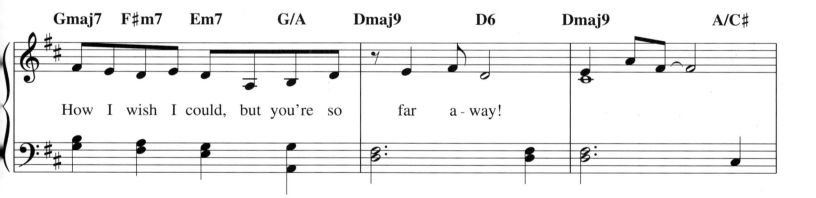

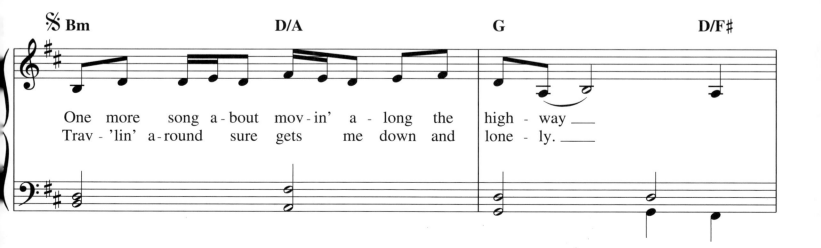

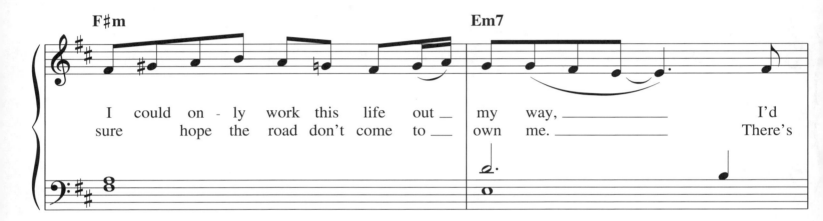

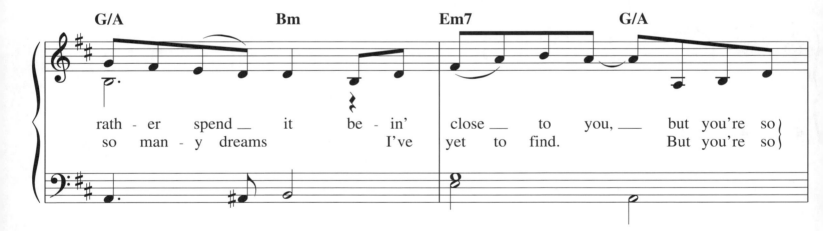

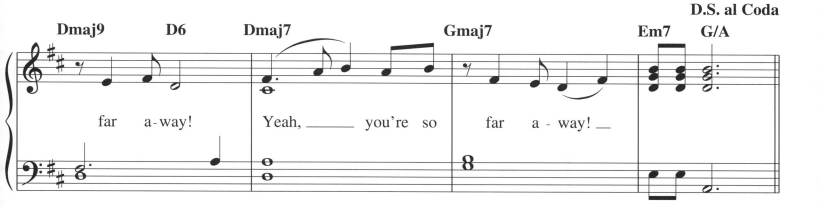

IT'S TOO LATE

Words and Music by CAROLE KING
and TONI STERN

Slowly

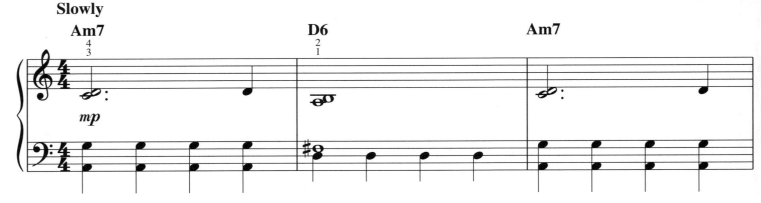

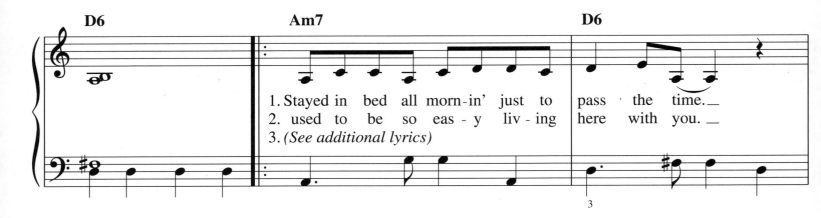

1. Stayed in bed all morn-in' just to pass the time. __
2. used to be so eas-y liv-ing here with you. __
3. *(See additional lyrics)*

There's some-thin' wrong here, there can be no de-ny - in'.
You were light and breez-y, and I knew just what to do. Now

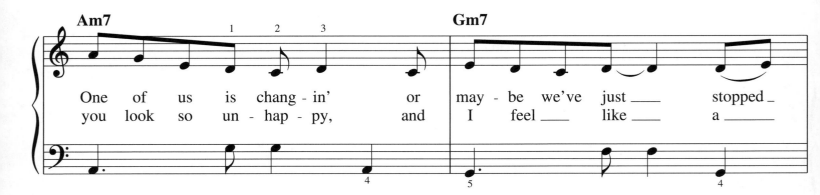

One of us is chang-in' or may-be we've just __ stopped __
you look so un-hap-py, and I feel __ like __ a __

Fmaj7

try - in'.
fool. _____

Chorus

B♭maj7

And it's   too late,   ba - by, now __

Fmaj7

it's too   late, __ though we

B♭maj7

real - ly did   try   to

Fmaj7

make it.

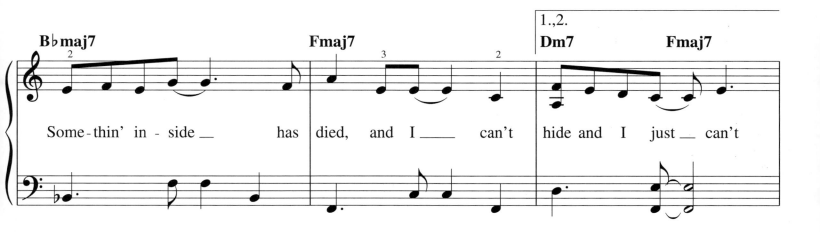

B♭maj7

Some-thin' in - side __   has

Fmaj7

died,   and I ____ can't

1.,2.

Dm7   Fmaj7

hide and I just __ can't

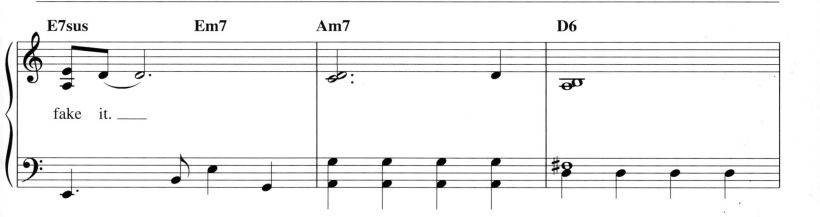

E7sus   Em7   Am7   D6

fake   it. ____

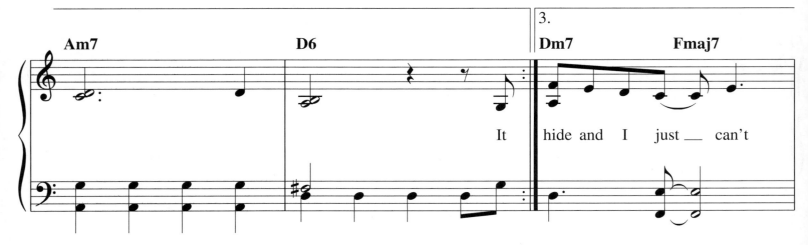

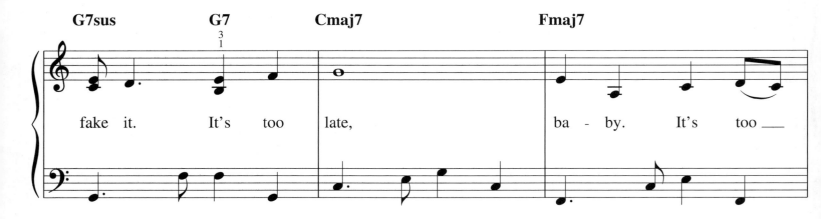

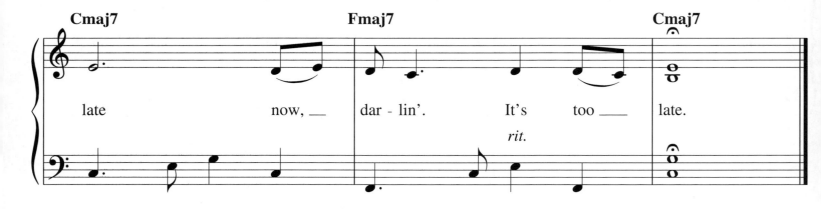

Additional Lyrics

3. There'll be good times again for me and you,
   But we just can't stay together.
   Don't you feel it, too?
   Still I'm glad for what we had
   And how I once loved you.
   Chorus

HOME AGAIN

Words and Music by
CAROLE KING

Slowly

Some - times I won - der if I'm

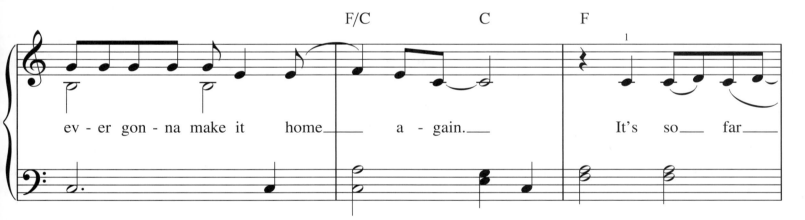

ev - er gon - na make it home___ a - gain.___ It's so___ far

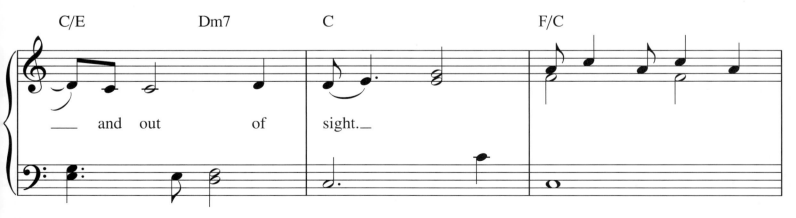

___ and out of sight.___

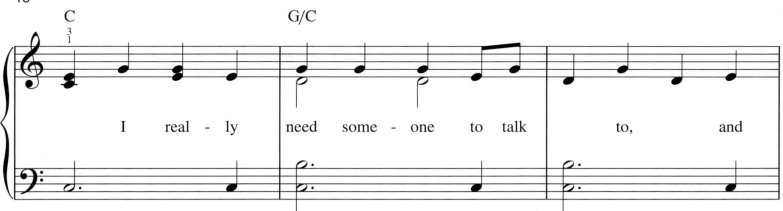

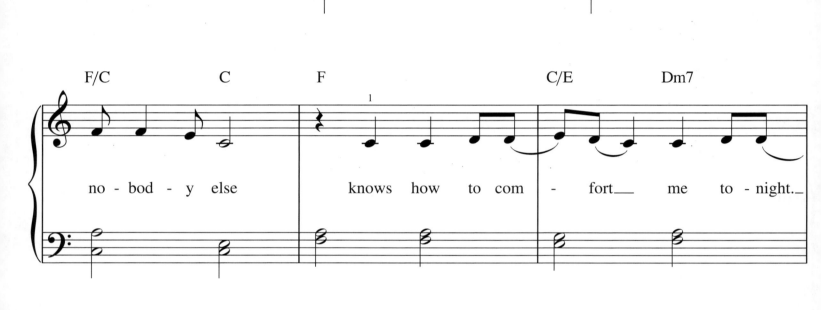

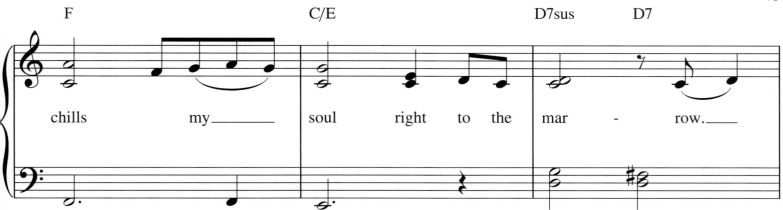

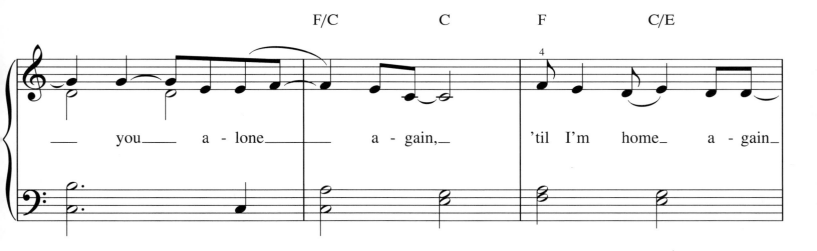

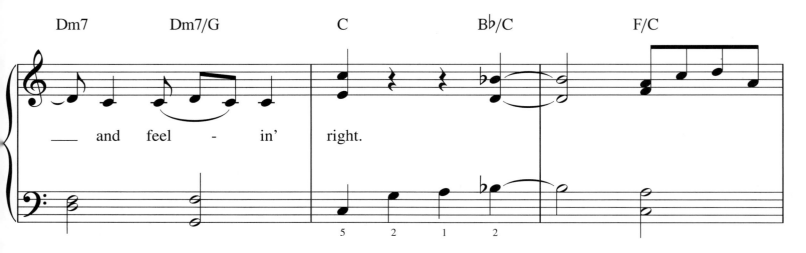

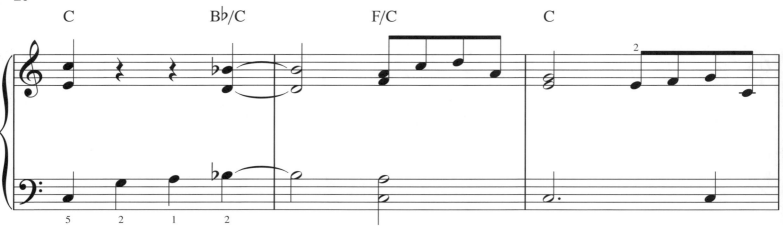

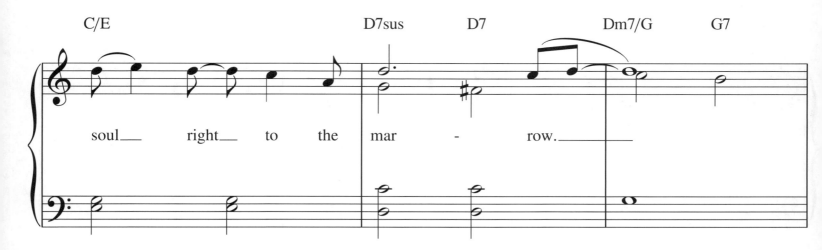

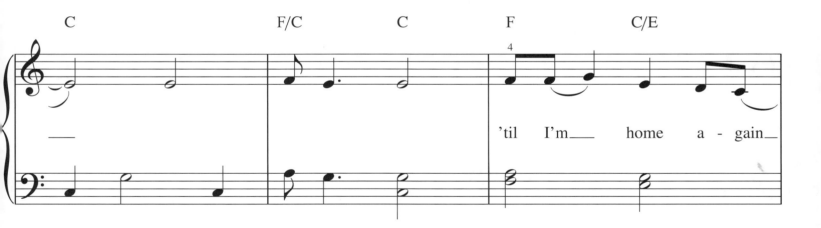

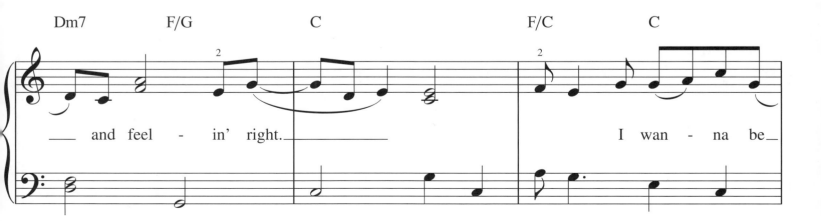

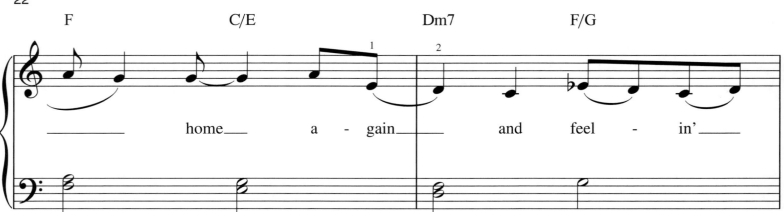

home__ a - gain__ and feel - in'__

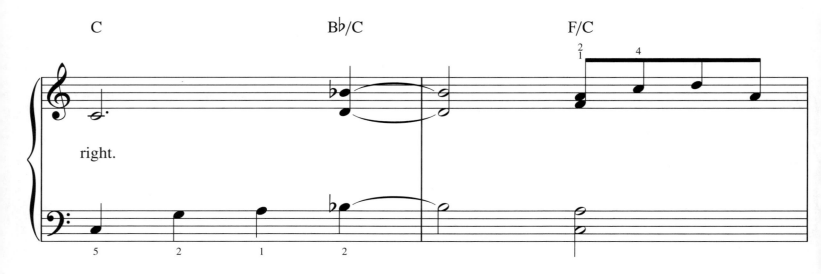

right.

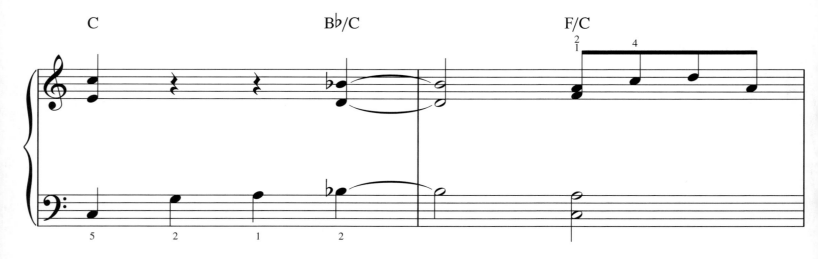

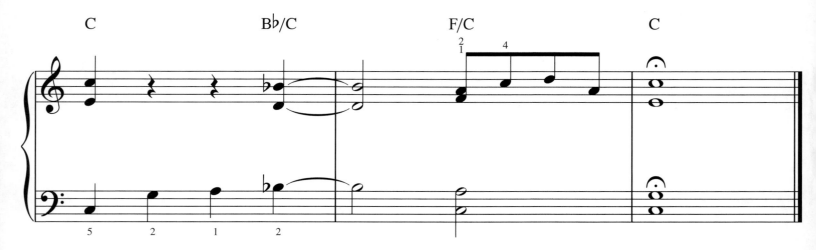

BEAUTIFUL

Words and Music by
CAROLE KING

Moderately slow

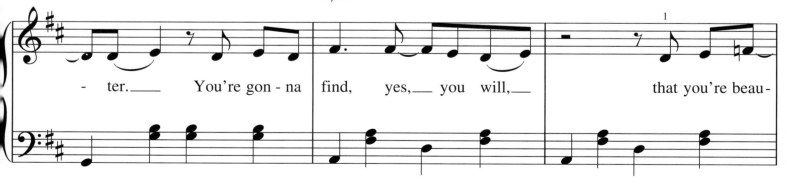

24

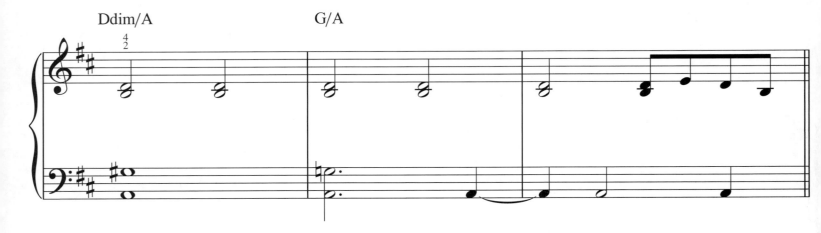

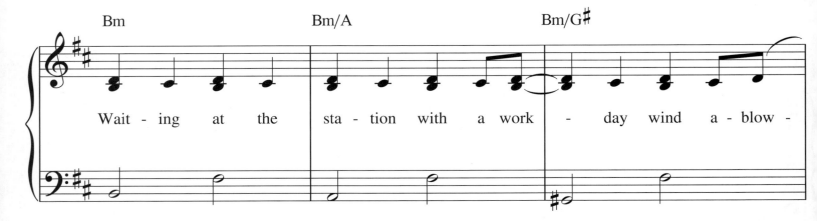

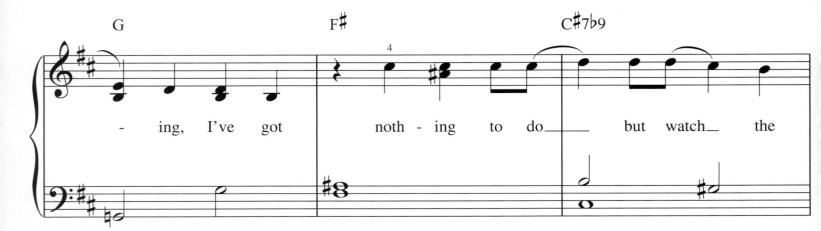

F#   Em7

passers - by.   Mir - rored in their

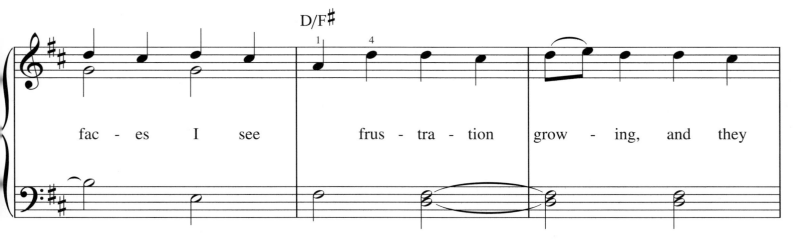

D/F#

fac - es I see   frus - tra - tion grow - ing, and they

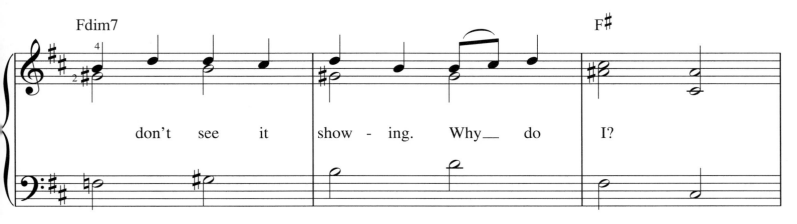

Fdim7   F#

don't see it   show - ing. Why__ do   I?

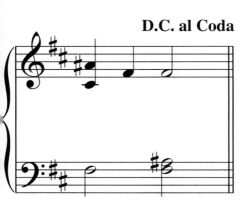

D.C. al Coda

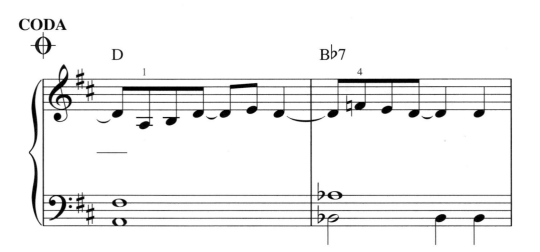

CODA

D   Bb7

I have of - ten asked____ my - self the rea -

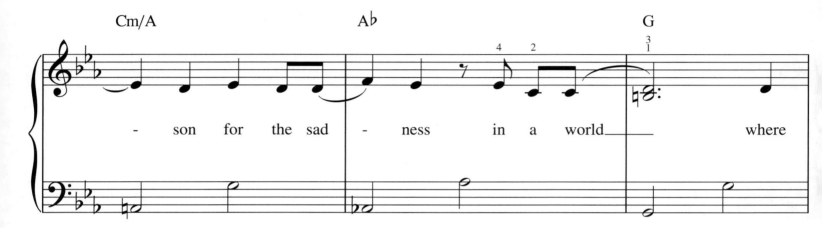

- son for the sad - ness in a world____ where

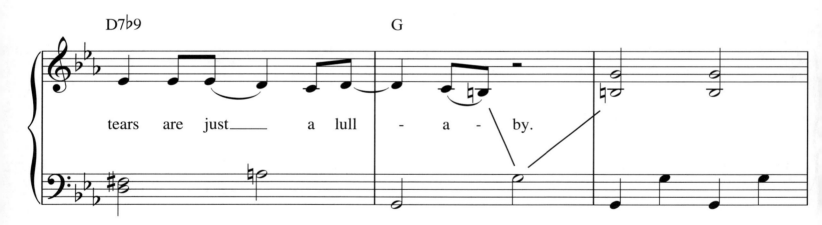

tears are just____ a lull - a - by.

If there's an - y an - swer, may - be love____ can end____ the mad -

- ness. May - be not, oh, but we___ can on - ly

try. You've got to

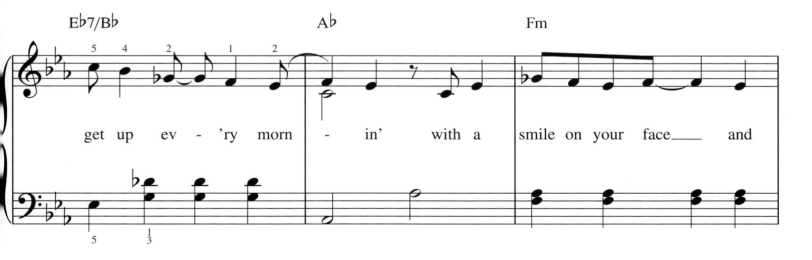

get up ev - 'ry morn - in' with a smile on your face___ and

show the world___ all___ the love___ in your heart._____

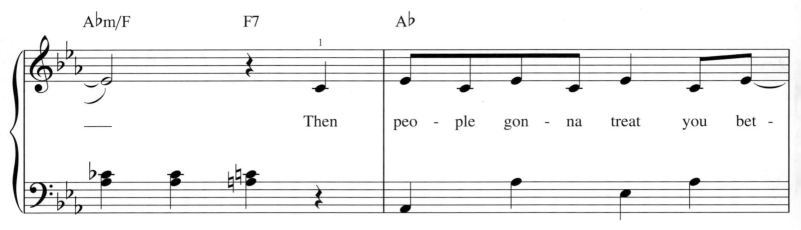

F#dim

you're beau - ti - ful

Eb/Bb

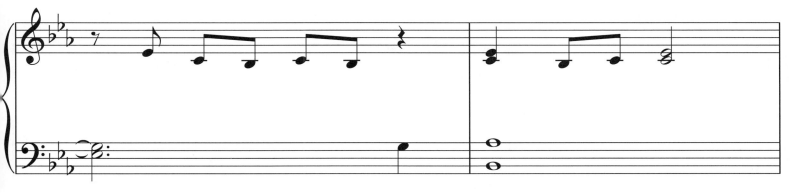

as you feel.

Ab/Bb

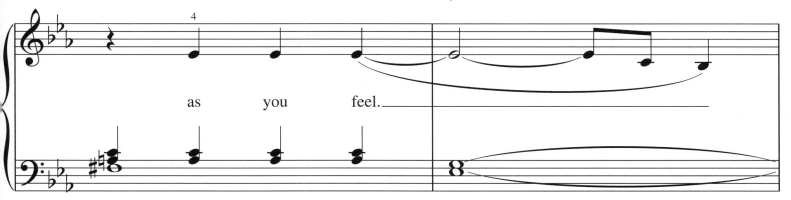

Eb

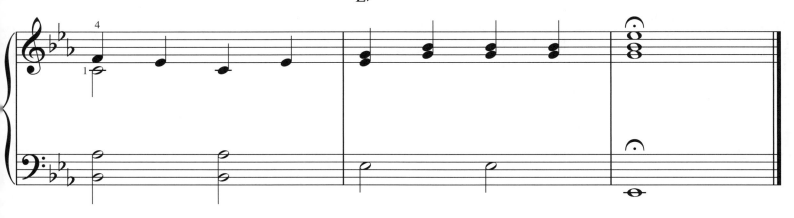

WAY OVER YONDER

Moderately slow

Words and Music by
CAROLE KING

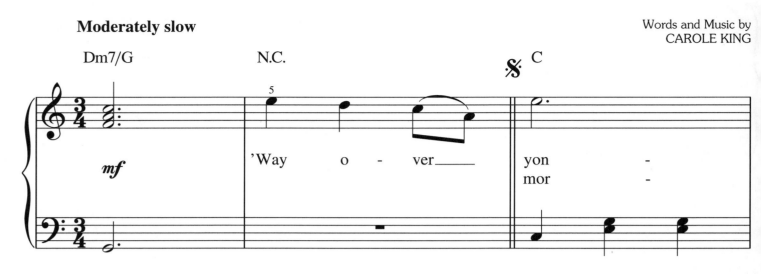

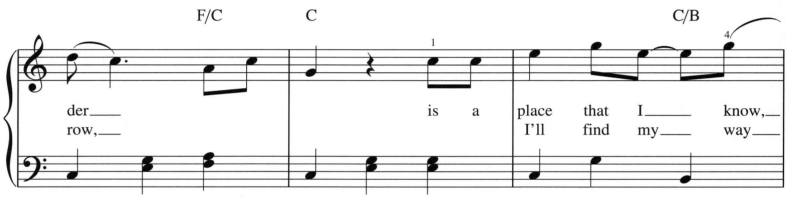

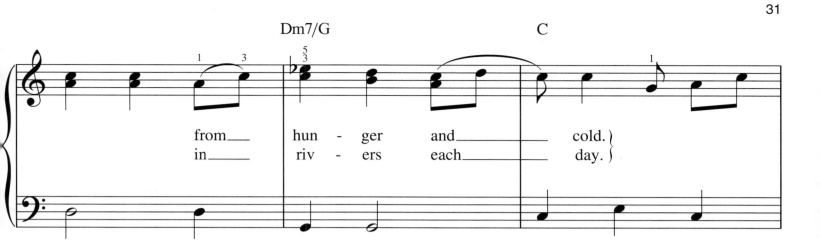

from____ hun - ger and_____ cold.
in____ riv - ers each_____ day.

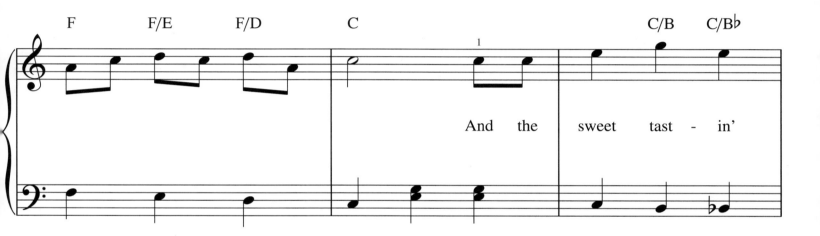

And the sweet tast - in'

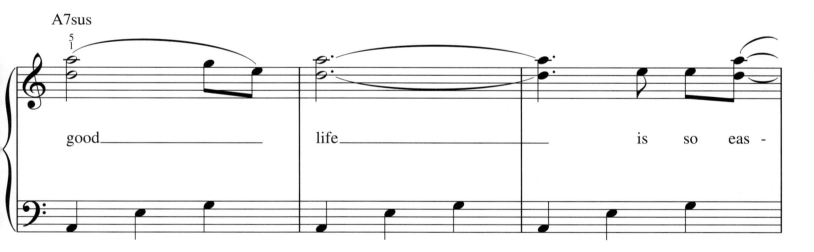

good_____ life_____ is so eas -

- i - ly found.____

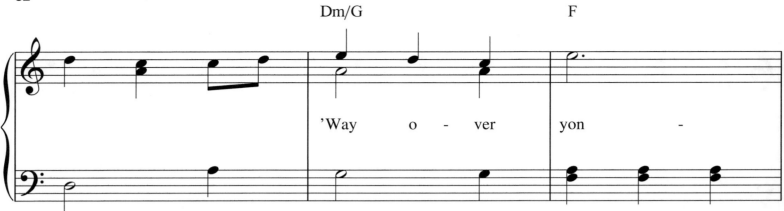

Dm/G   F

'Way   o - ver   yon -

F/G

der,_____   that's   where   I'm____

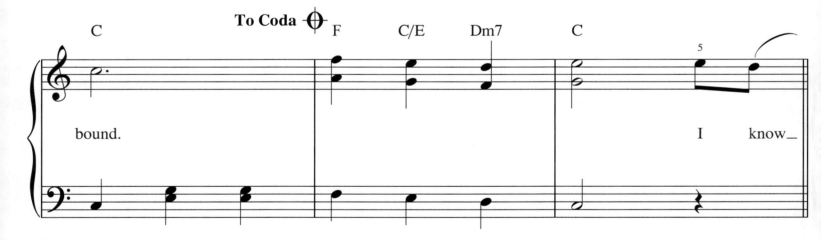

To Coda ⊕

C   F   C/E   Dm7   C

bound.   I   know_

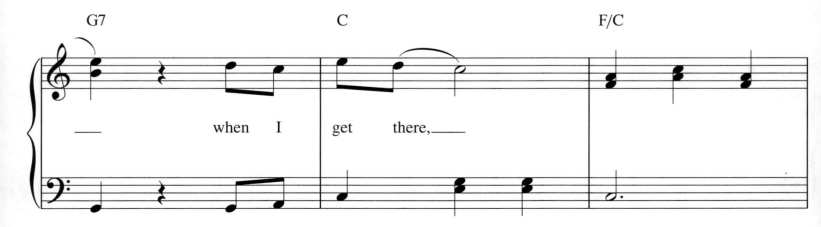

G7   C   F/C

_   when   I   get   there,____

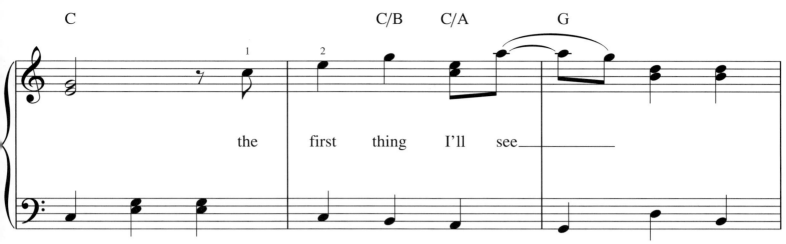

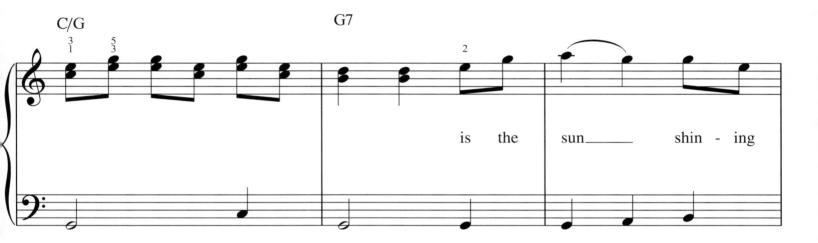

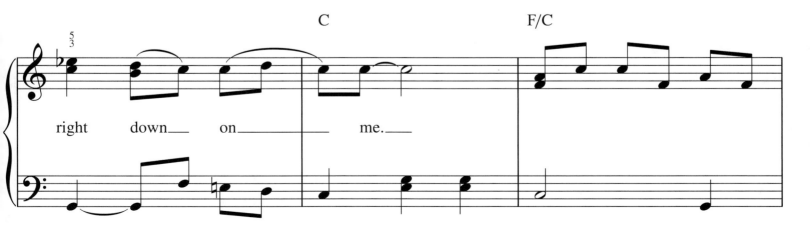

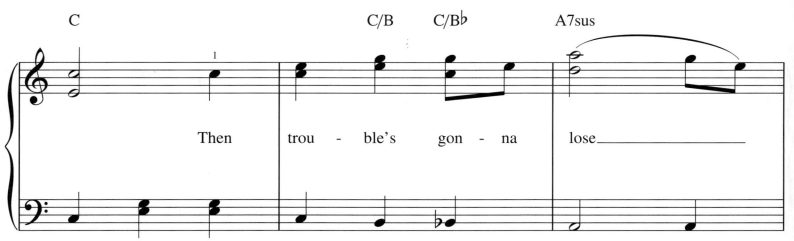

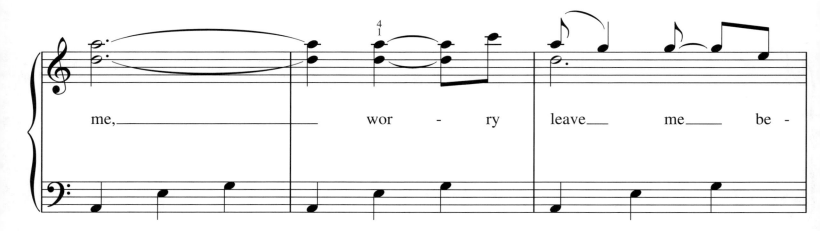

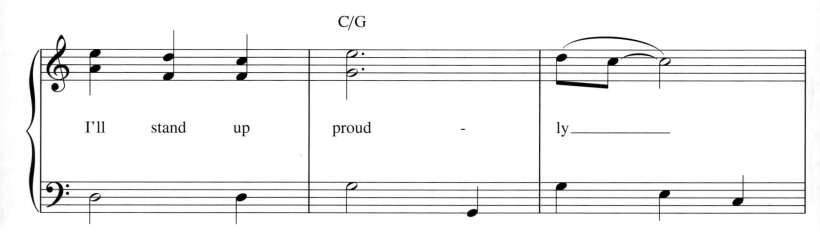

in   true   peace   of   mind.

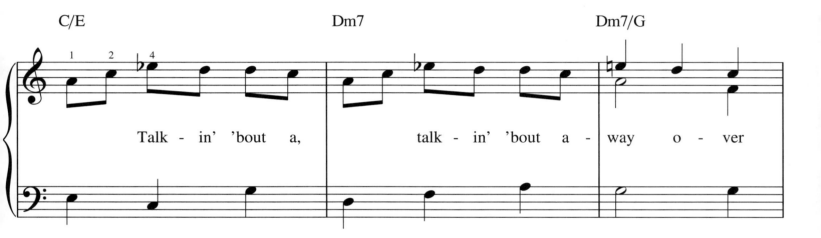

Talk - in' 'bout a,   talk - in' 'bout a - way   o - ver

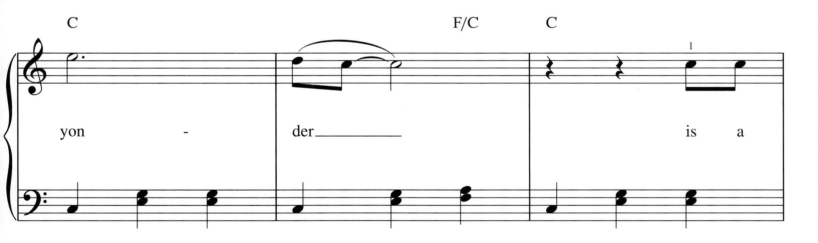

yon -   der_____   is   a

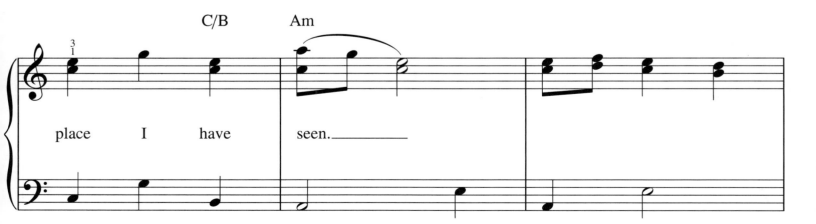

place   I   have   seen._____

It's a gar - den of wis - dom

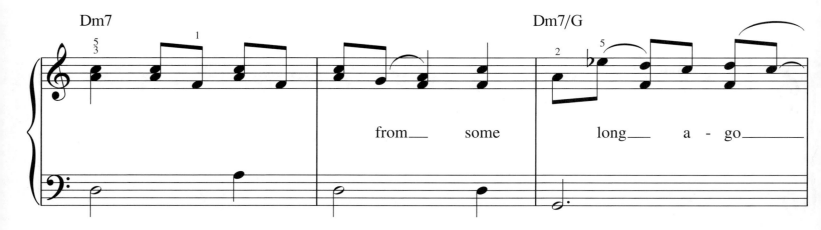

from some long a - go

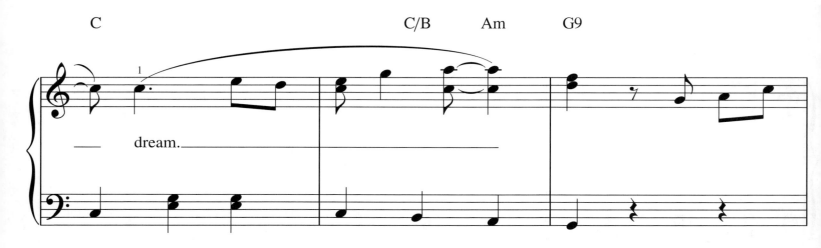

dream.

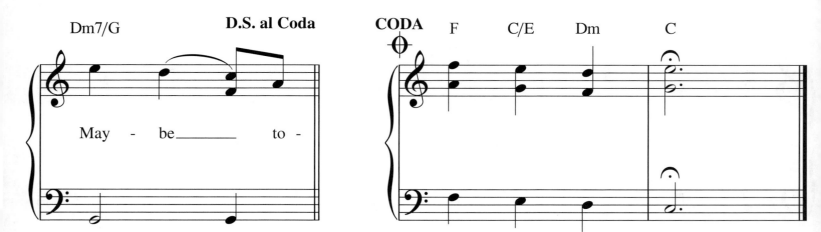

May - be to -

YOU'VE GOT A FRIEND

Words and Music by
CAROLE KING

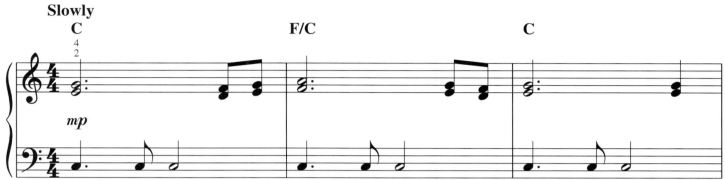

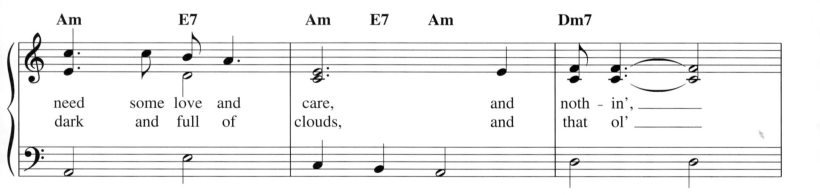

When you're | down | and trou - bled | and you
sky | a - bove __ | you | grows __

need | some love and | care, | and | noth - in', _____
dark | and full of | clouds, | and | that ol' _____

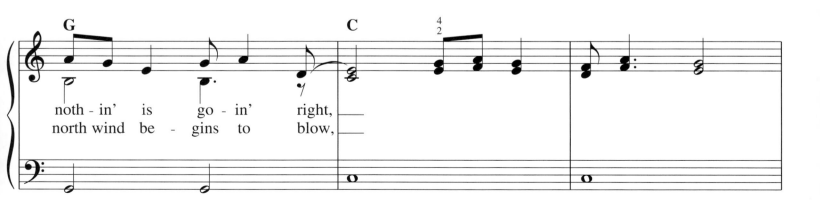

noth - in' is | go - in' | right, _____
north wind be - gins to | blow, _____

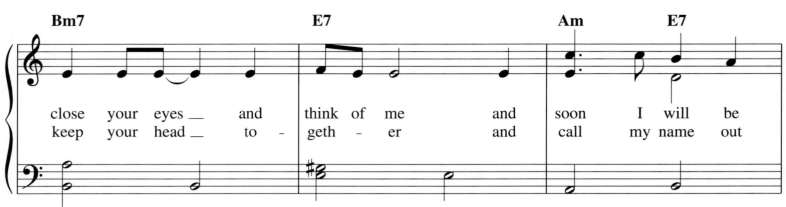

close your eyes __ and | think of me and | soon I will be
keep your head __ to - | geth - er and | call my name out

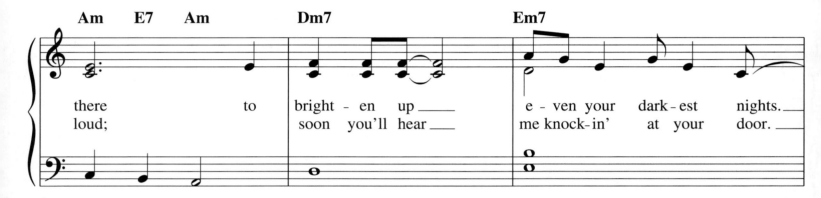

there to | bright - en up __ | e - ven your dark - est nights. __
loud; | soon you'll hear __ | me knock - in' at your door. __

You just | call out my __ name __

__ | and you know wher - ev - er I | am I'll come run -

-nin' to see you a-gain.

Win-ter, spring, sum-mer and fall,

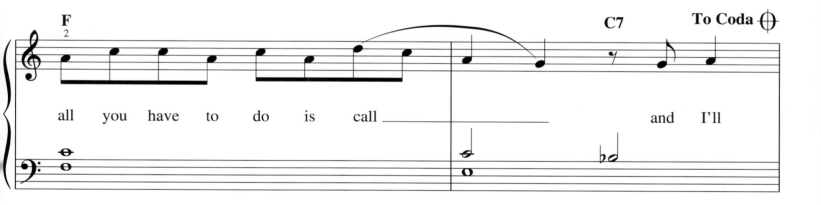

all you have to do is call and I'll

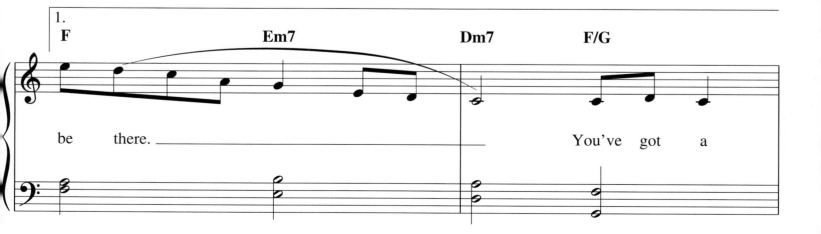

be there. You've got a

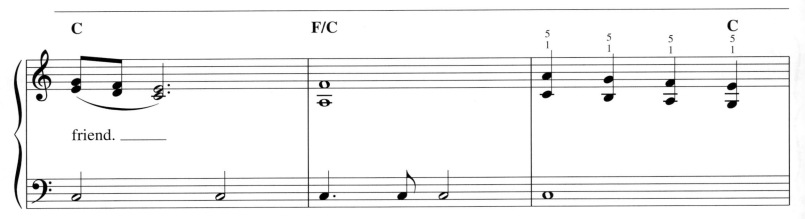

C   F/C   C

friend. _____

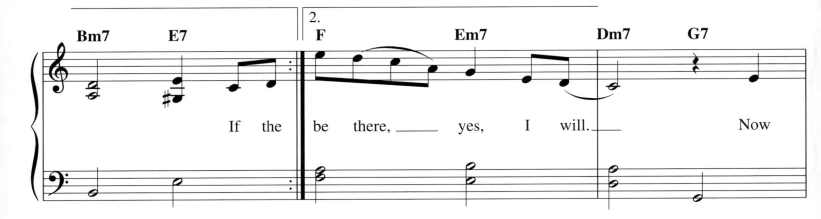

Bm7   E7   2.   F   Em7   Dm7   G7

If the   be there, _____ yes,   I   will.____   Now

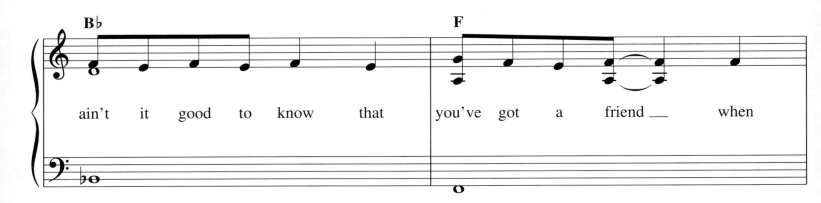

B♭   F

ain't it good to know that   you've got a   friend __ when

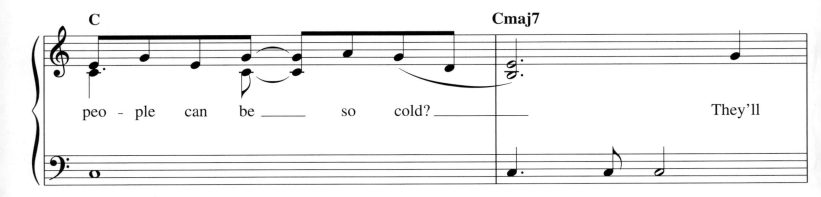

C   Cmaj7

peo - ple can be _____ so cold? _____   They'll

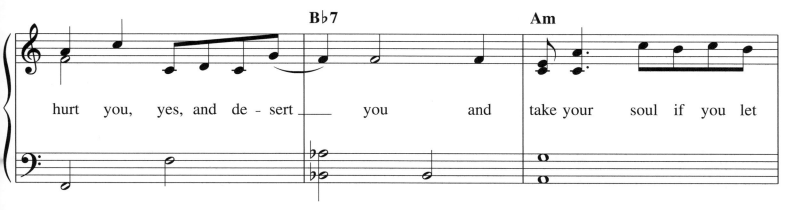

hurt you, yes, and de - sert ___ you and take your soul if you let

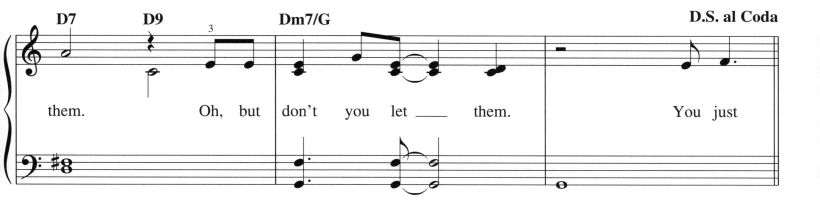

them. Oh, but don't you let ___ them. You just

CODA

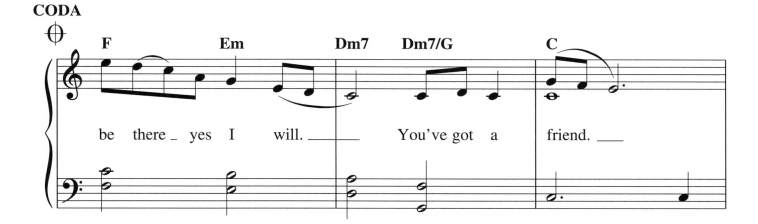

be there _ yes I will. ___ You've got a friend. ___

You've got a friend. ___ Ain't it good to know you've got a

WHERE YOU LEAD

Words and Music by CAROLE KING
and TONI STERN

Moderately

Want - ing you the way I do,_____ I
If you're out on the road,_____

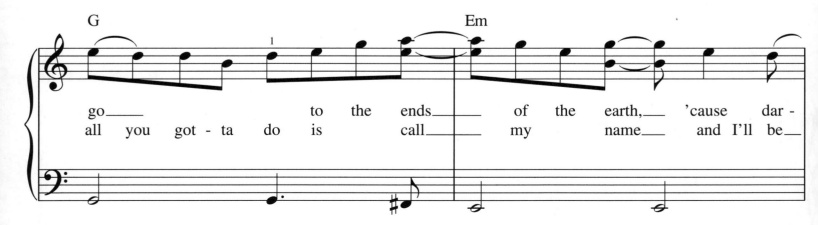

on - ly want to be with_____ you._____ And I would
feel - in' lone - ly and so_____ cold,_____

go_____ to the ends_____ of the earth, 'cause dar-
all you got - ta do is call_____ my name_____ and I'll be

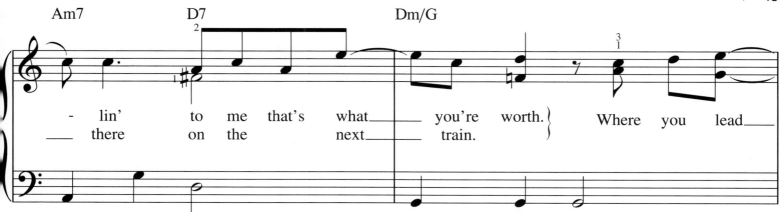

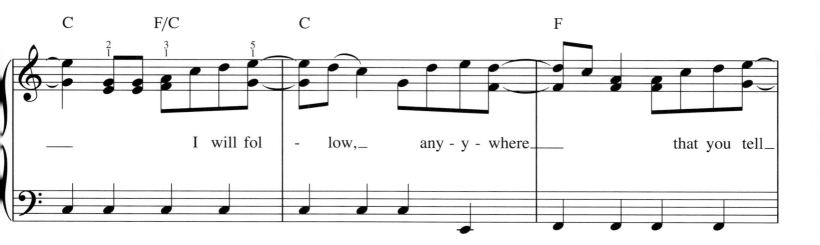

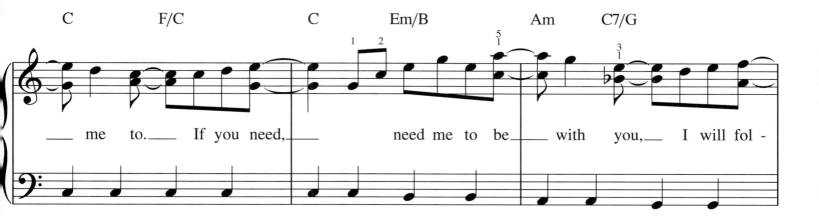

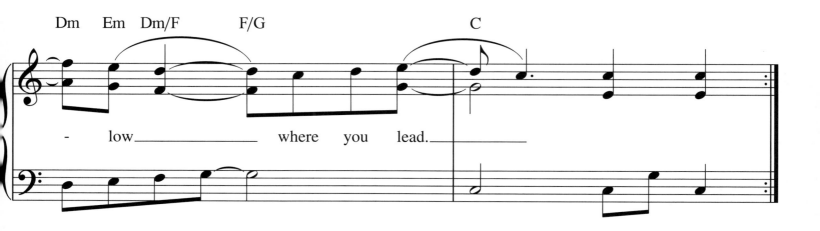

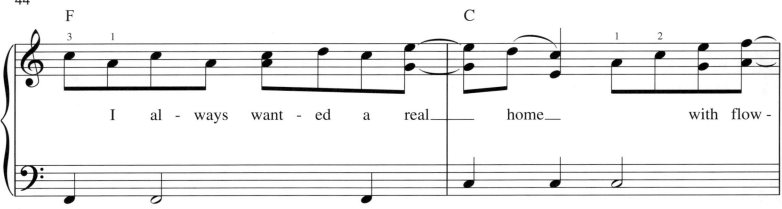

I al - ways want - ed a real___ home___ with flow-

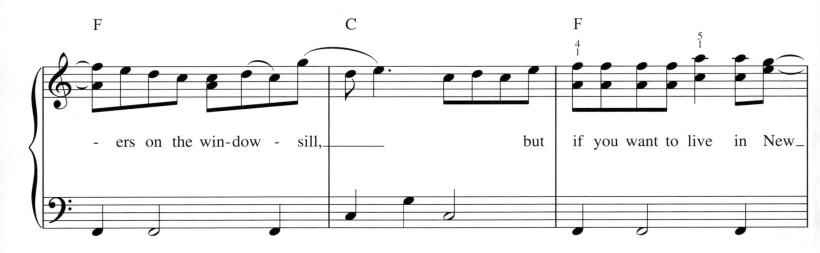

- ers on the win-dow - sill,_____ but if you want to live in New_

___ York_ Cit - y,___ hon - ey, you know_ I ___ will.___

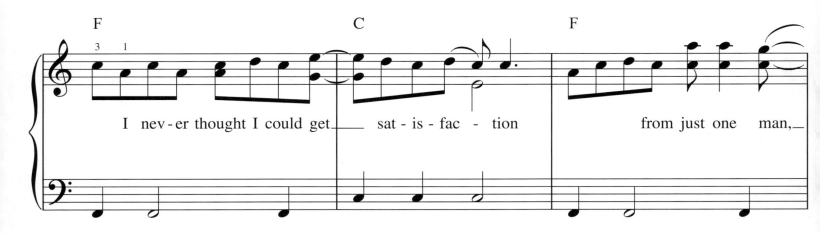

I nev - er thought I could get___ sat - is - fac - tion from just one man,_

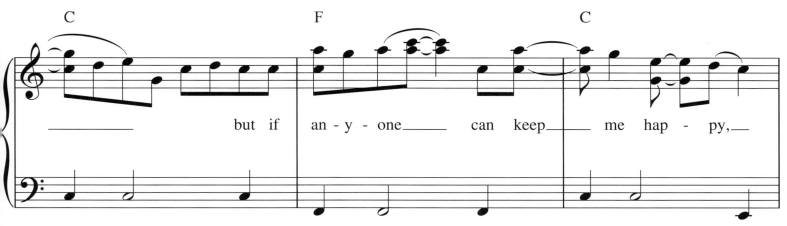

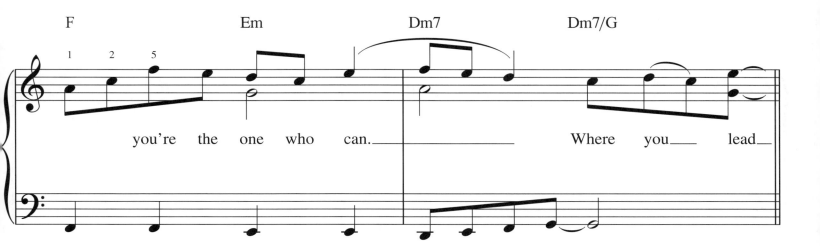

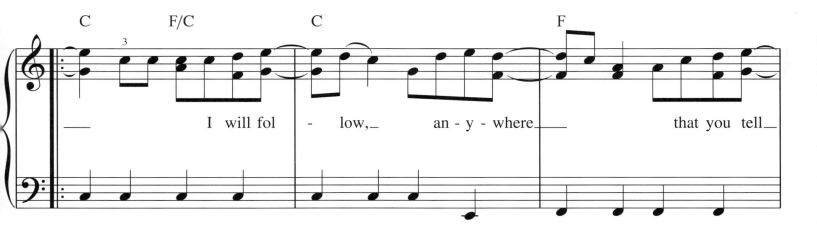

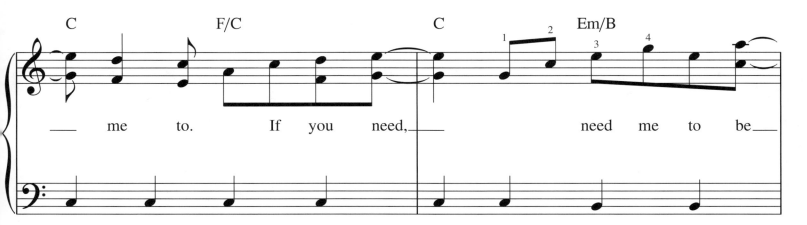

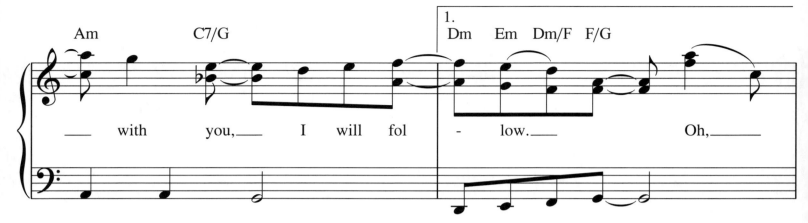

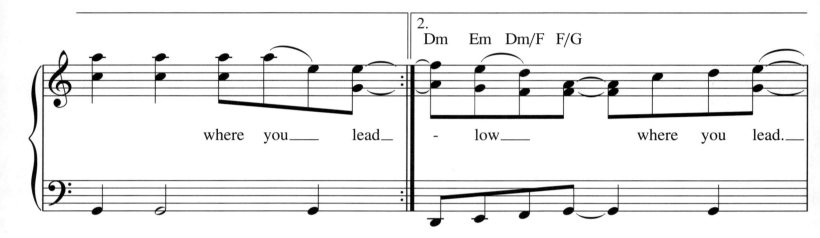

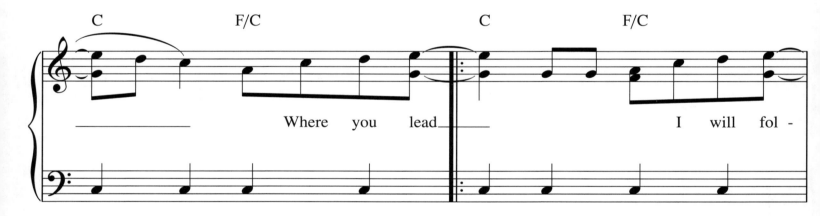

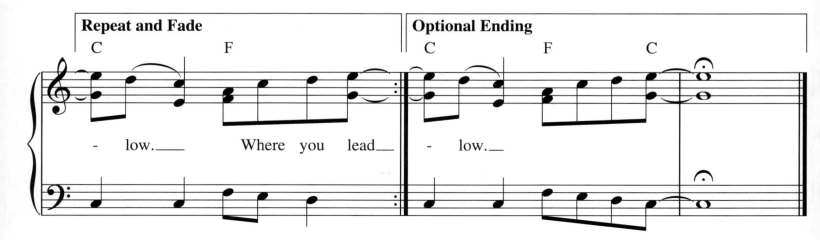

WILL YOU LOVE ME TOMORROW

(Will You Still Love Me Tomorrow)

Words and Music by GERRY GOFFIN
and CAROLE KING

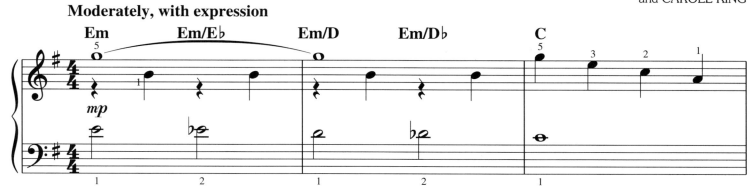

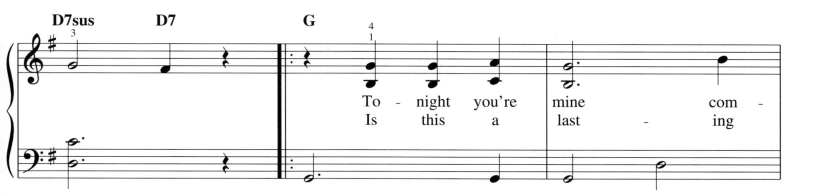

To - night you're mine coming
Is this a last - ing

plete - ly, you give your
treas - ure, or just a

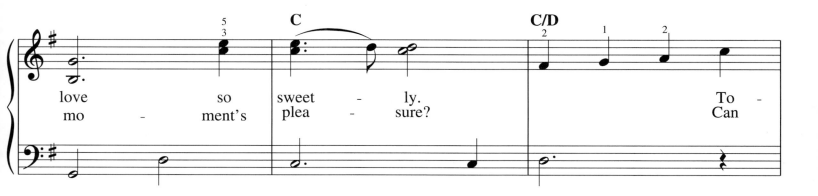

love so sweet - ly. To -
mo - ment's plea - sure? Can

48

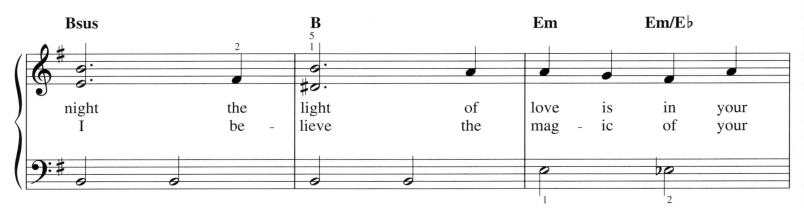

night   the   light   of   the   love   is   in   your

I   be -   lieve   the   mag -   ic   of   your

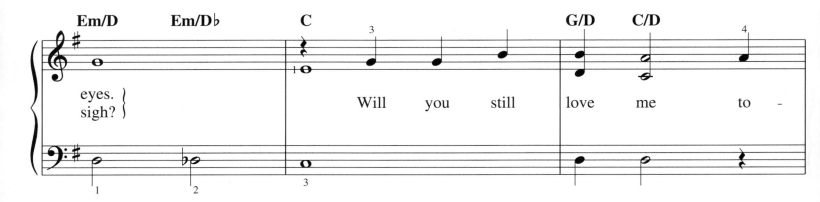

eyes. }
sigh? }   Will   you   still   love   me   to -

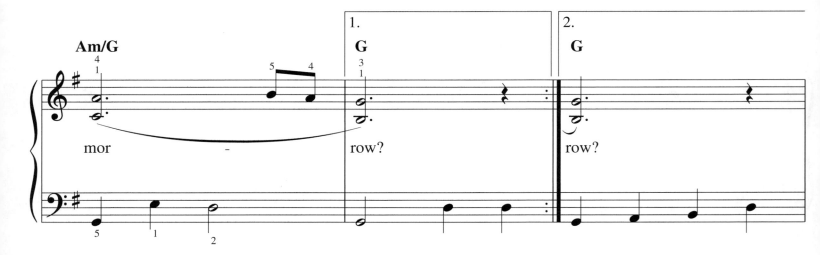

mor -   row?   row?

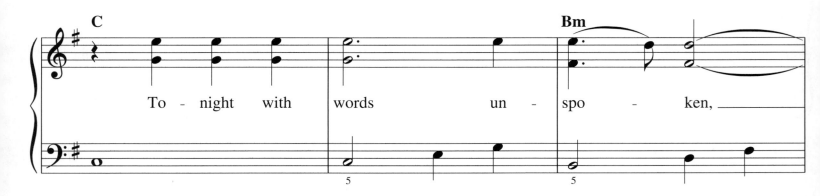

To - night   with   words   un - spo - ken, _____

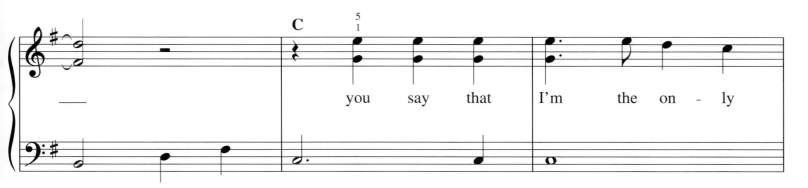

you say that I'm the on - ly

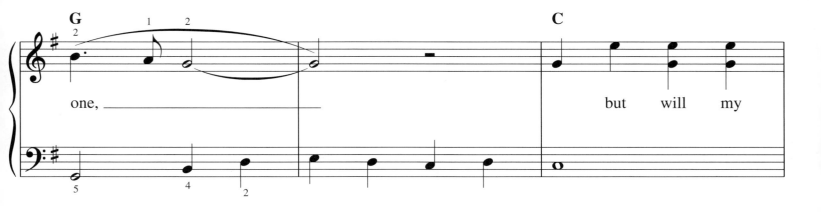

one, _____ but will my

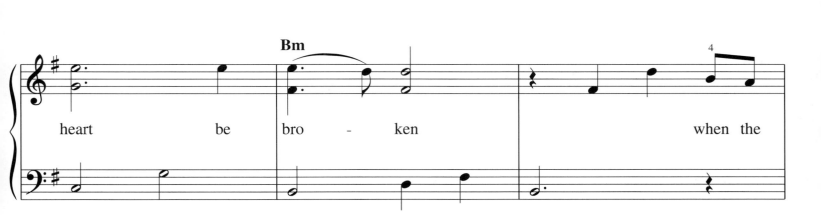

heart be bro - ken when the

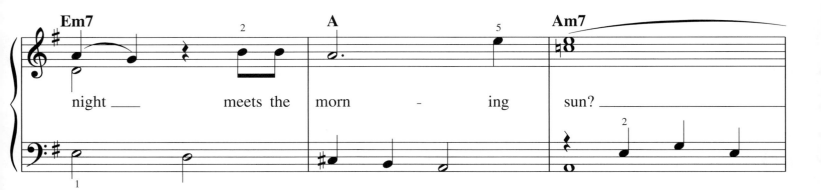

night ___ meets the morn - ing sun? _____

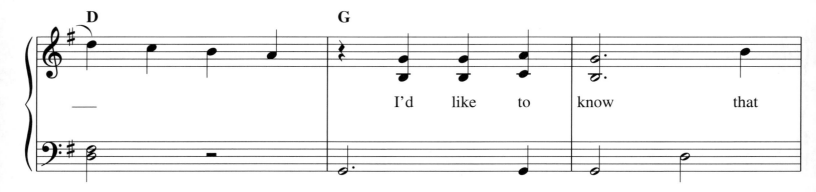

I'd like to know that

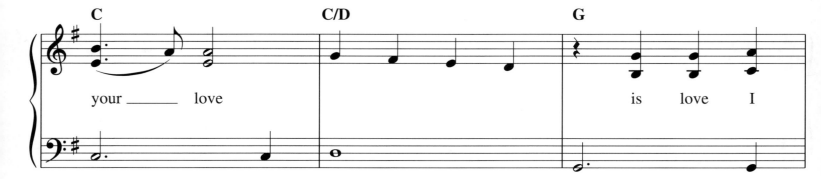

your _____ love   is love I

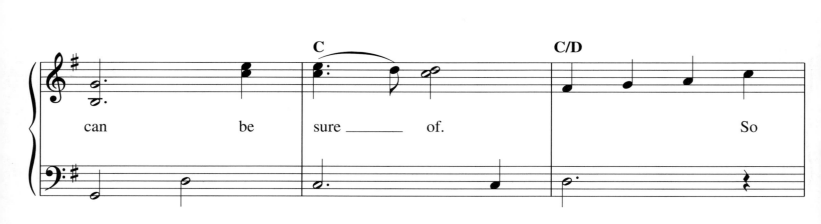

can   be   sure _____ of.   So

tell   me   now   and   I   won't   ask   a -

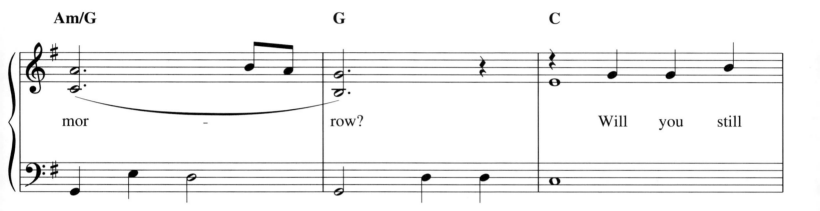

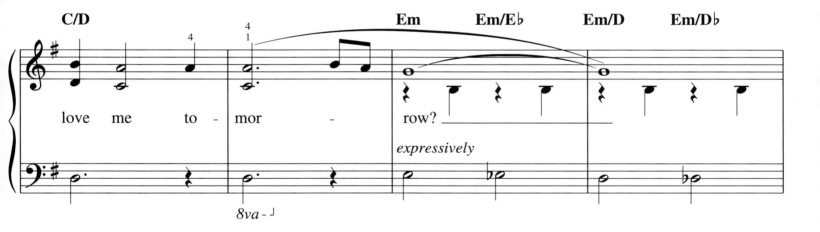

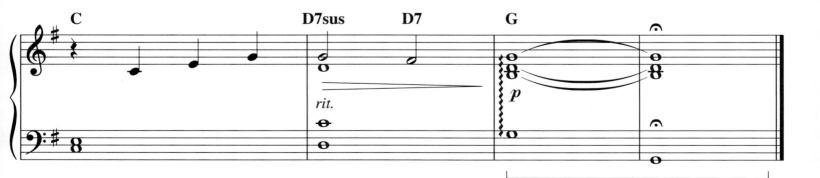

SMACKWATER JACK

Words and Music by GERRY GOFFIN
and CAROLE KING

Moderate Swing

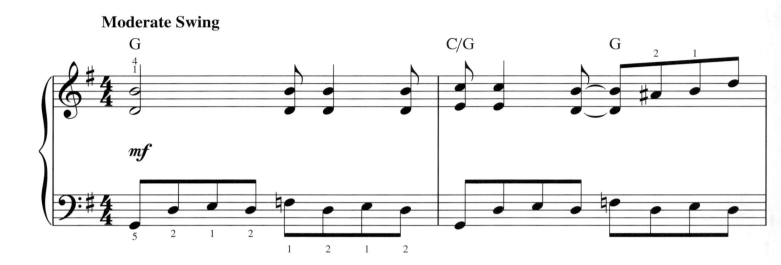

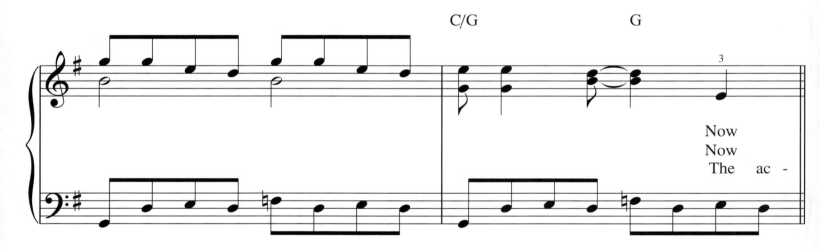

Now
Now
The ac -

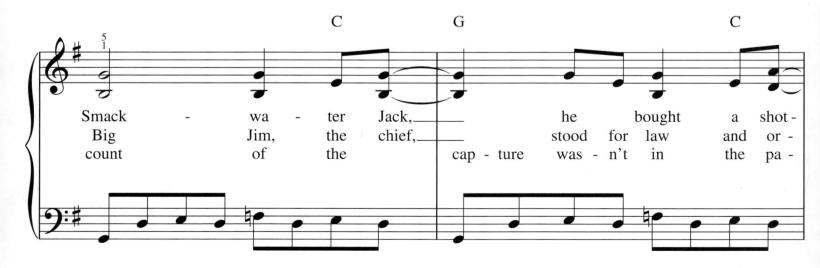

Smack - wa - ter Jack,___ he bought a shot-
Big Jim, the chief,___ stood for law and or-
count of the cap - ture was - n't in the pa -

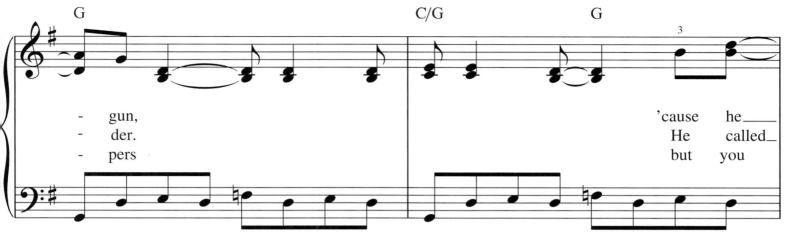

- gun,
- der.
- pers

'cause he____
He called____
but you

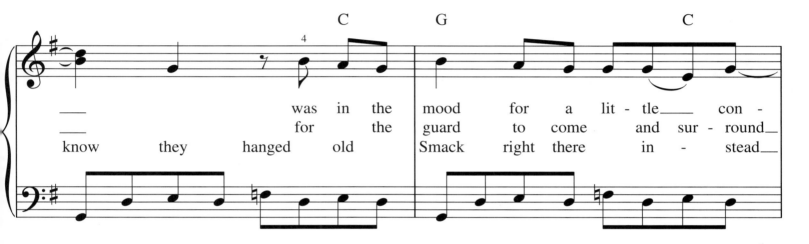

____
____
know they hanged old

was in the
for the
Smack

mood
guard
right

for
to
there

a
come
in -

lit - tle____ con -
and sur - round____
stead____

- fron - ta - tion.____
____ the bor - der.____
____ of lat - er.____

He just - a
You know the

let it all____ hang loose,____ ____
From his bull - dog mouth,____
peo - ple were____ quite pleased,____

he did - n't
as he
'cause the

think a - bout___ the noose;___ he could - n't
led the pos - se south,___ came the
out - law had___ been seized___ and on the

To Coda ⊕

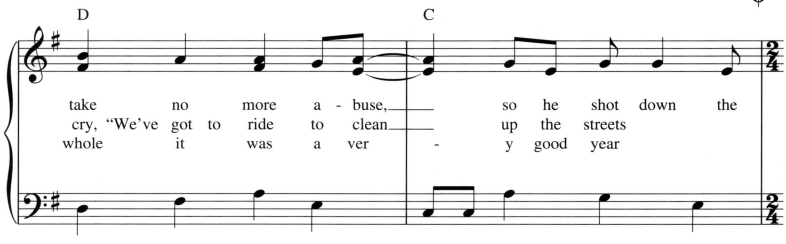

take no more a - buse,___ so he shot down the
cry, "We've got to ride to clean___ up the streets
whole it was a ver - y good year

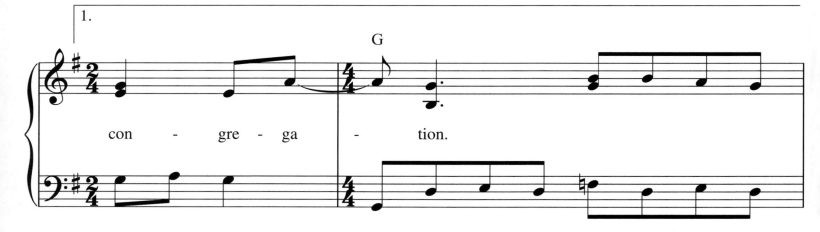

con - gre - ga - tion.

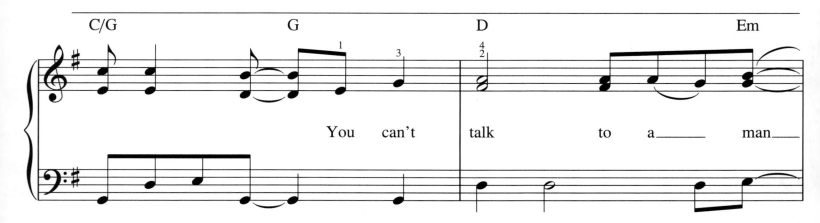

You can't talk to a___ man___

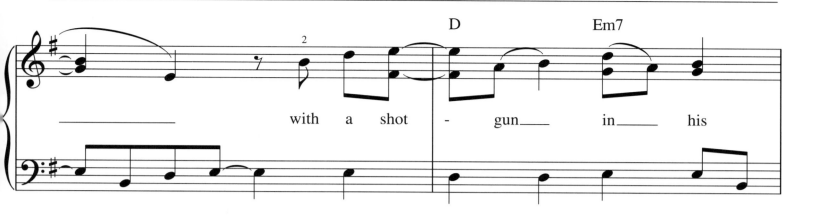

with a shot - gun___ in___ his

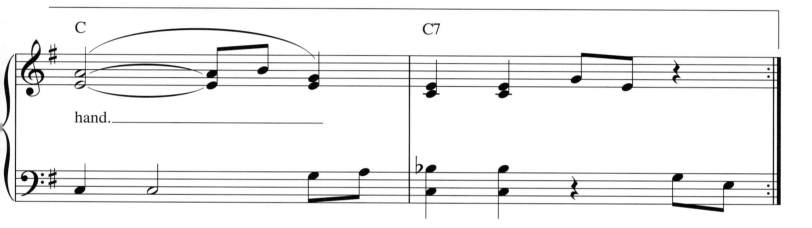

hand.___

for our wives___ and our daugh - ters."

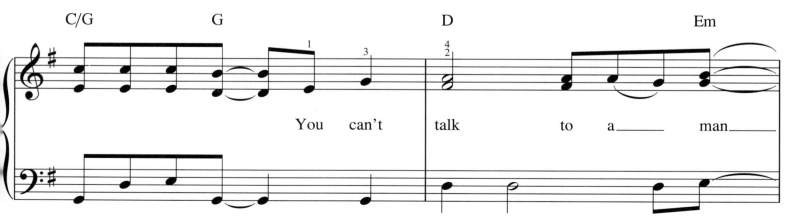

You can't talk to a___ man___

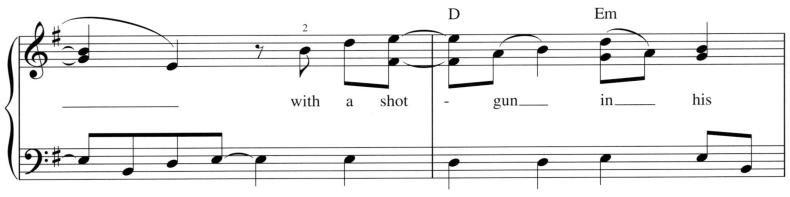

with a shot - gun___ in___ his

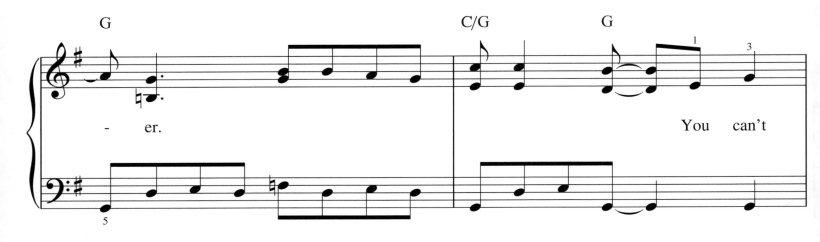

hand.___

D.C. al Coda

CODA

for the un - der - tak -

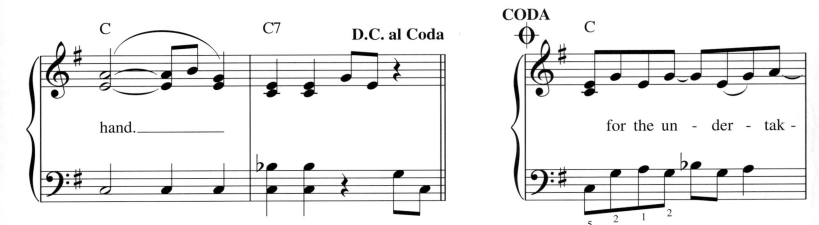

- er.

You can't

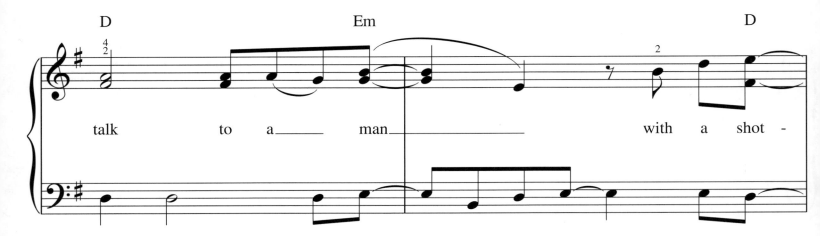

talk to a___ man___ with a shot -

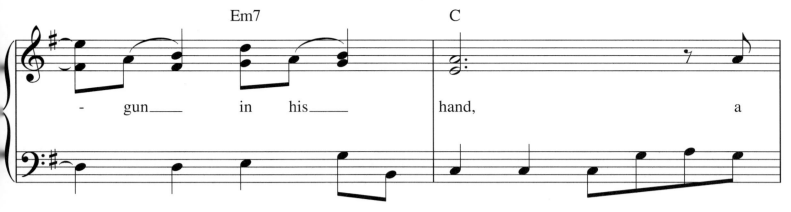

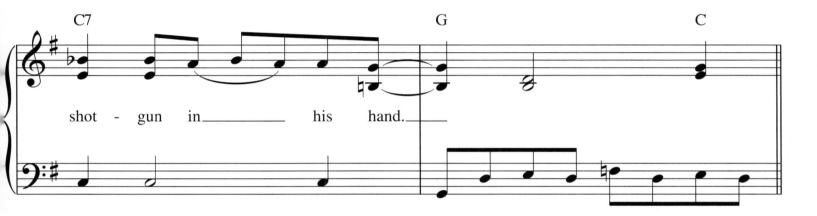

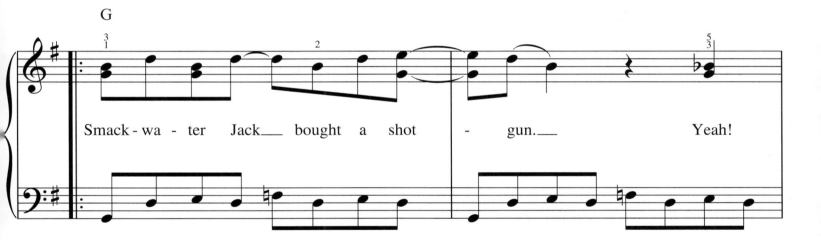

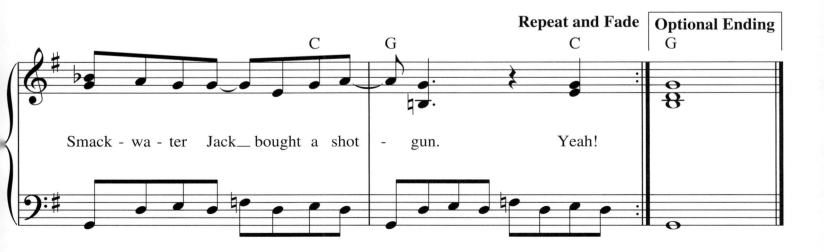

TAPESTRY

Words and Music by
CAROLE KING

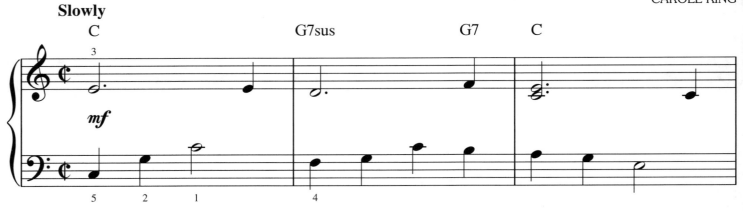

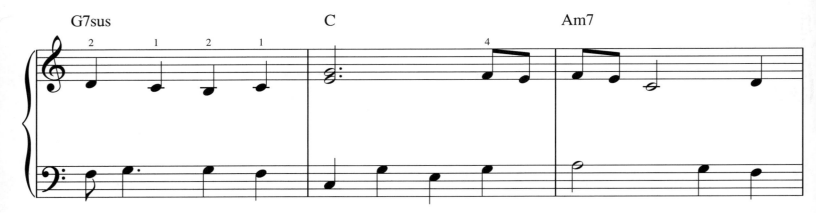

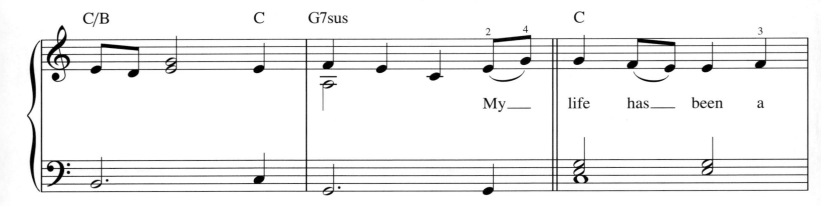

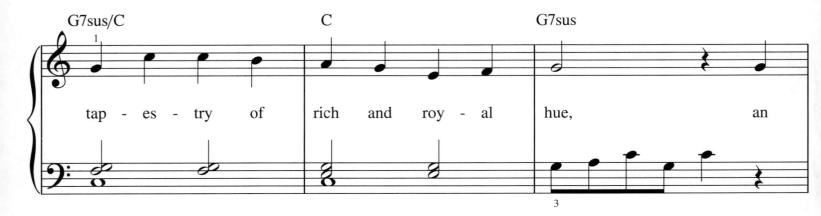

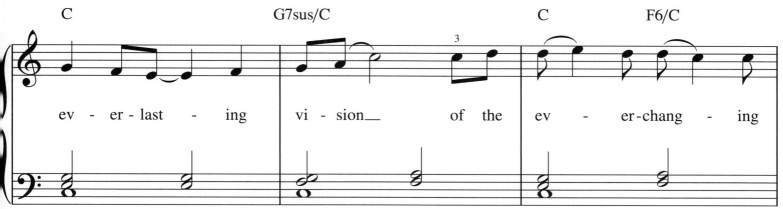

ev - er - last - ing   vi - sion____   of the   ev - er-chang - ing

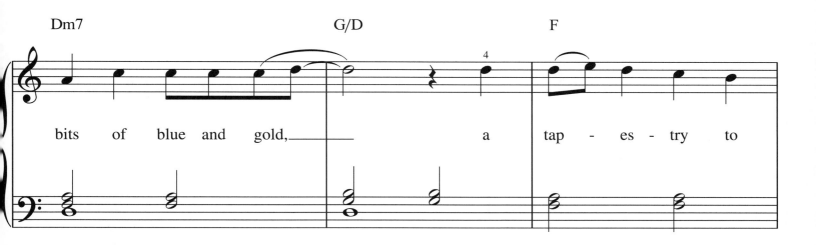

view,   a   won - d'rous wov - en   mag - ic   in

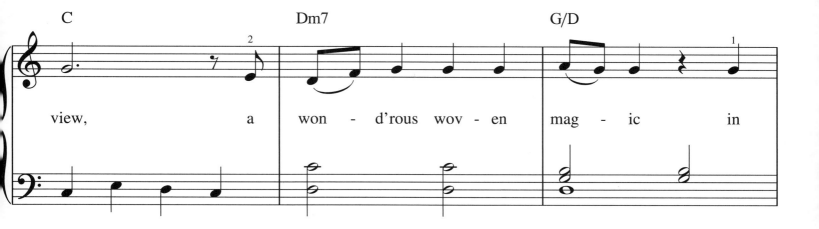

bits   of   blue   and   gold,____   a   tap - es - try   to

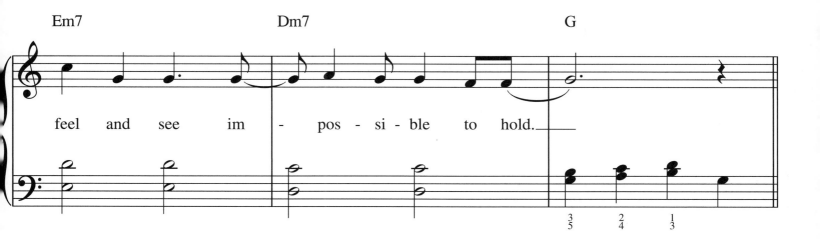

feel   and   see   im - pos - si - ble   to   hold.____

60

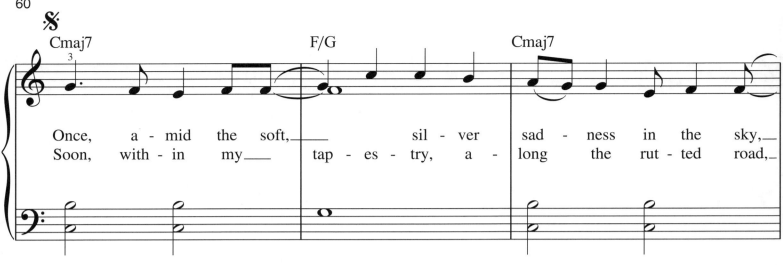

Cmaj7 / F/G / Cmaj7

Once, a - mid the soft,___ sil - ver sad - ness in the sky,
Soon, with - in my___ tap - es - try, a - long the rut - ted road,___

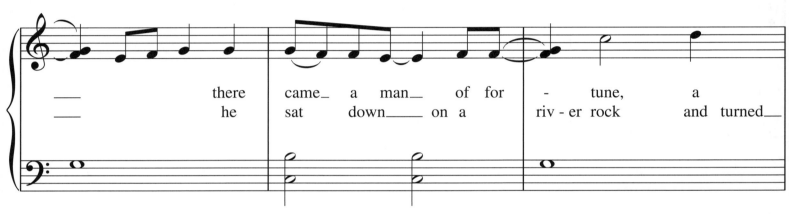

F/G / Cmaj7 / F/G

___ there came_ a man_ of for - tune, a
___ he sat down___ on a riv - er rock and turned___

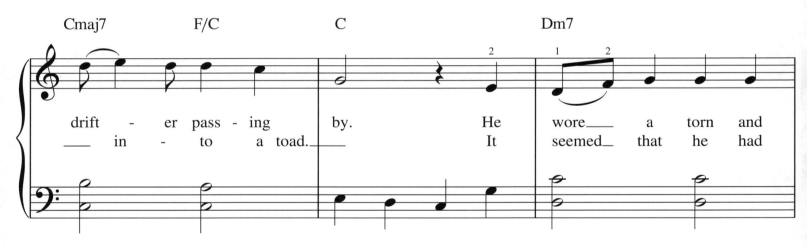

Cmaj7 / F/C / C / Dm7

drift - er pass - ing by. He wore___ a torn and
___ in - to a toad.___ It seemed_ that he had

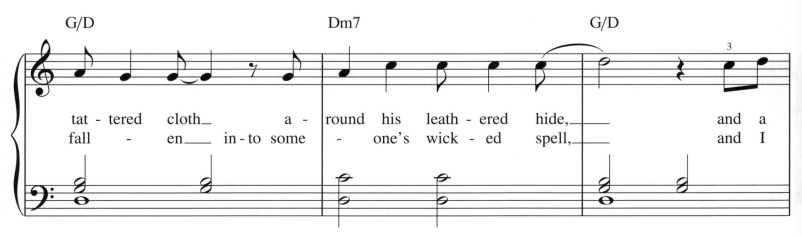

G/D / Dm7 / G/D

tat - tered cloth___ a - round his leath - ered hide,___ and a
fall - en___ in - to some - one's wick - ed spell,___ and I

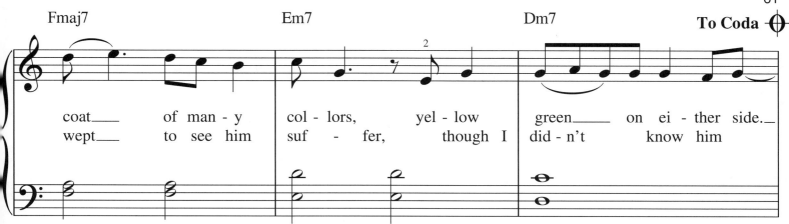

Fmaj7 Em7 Dm7 **To Coda** ⊕

coat____ of man - y | col - lors, yel - low | green____ on ei - ther side.____
wept____ to see him | suf - fer, though I | did - n't know him

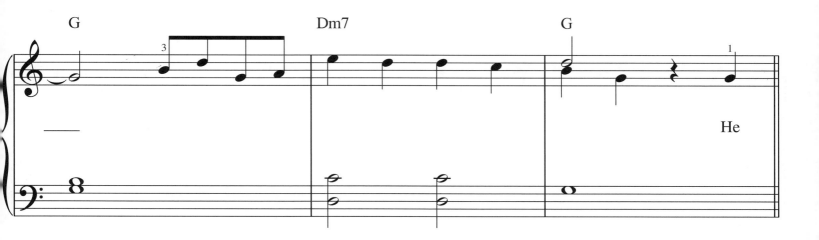

G Dm7 G

____

He

E♭ A♭/E♭ B♭/E♭

moved with__ some un - | cer - tain - ty, as | if he did - n't

A♭/E♭ E♭ A♭/E♭

know | just what he was there____ for,____ or____

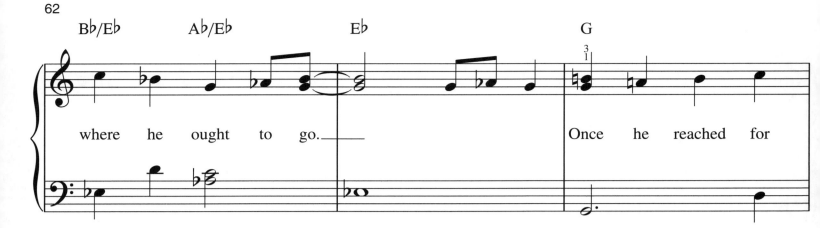

where he ought to go. ____ Once he reached for

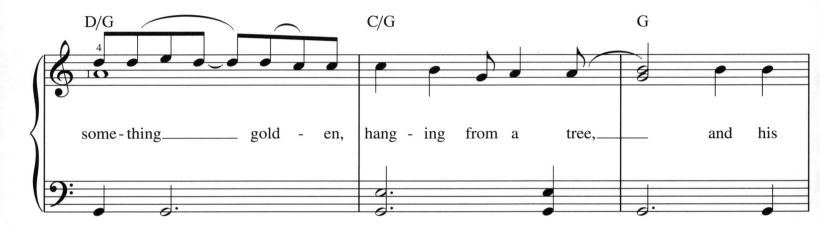

some-thing _____ gold - en, hang - ing from a tree, ____ and his

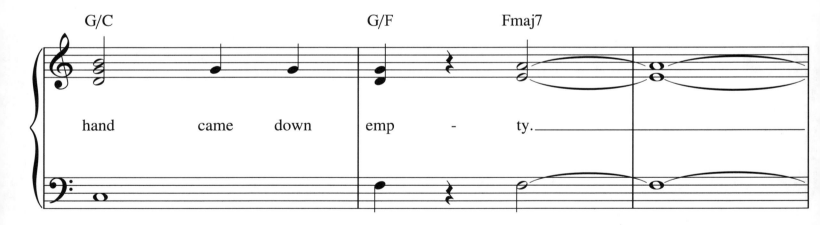

hand came down emp - ty. ____

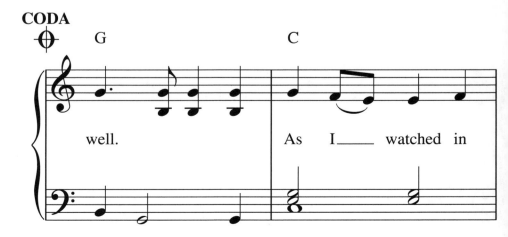

____ well. As I ____ watched in

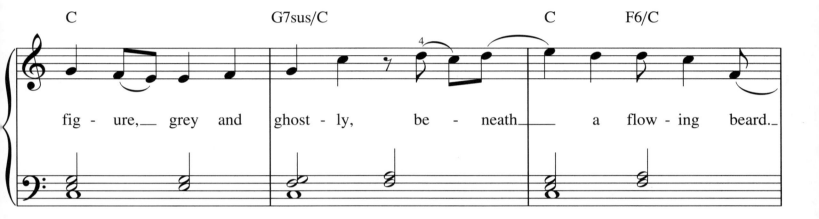

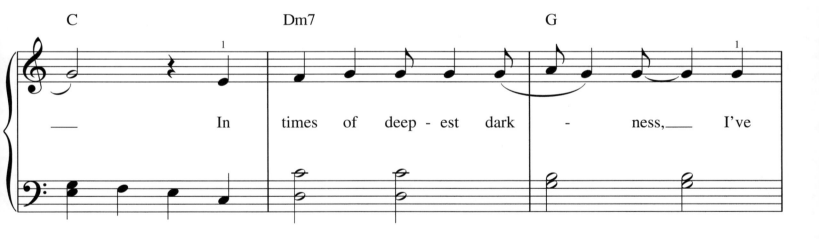

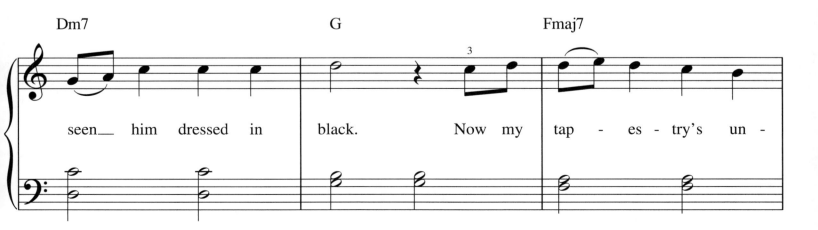

Em7   Dm7   G

rav - el - ing; he's   come_____ to take me   back.   He's

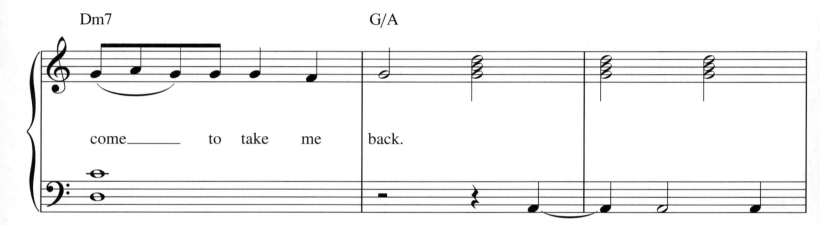

Dm7   G/A

come_____ to take me   back.

F/G

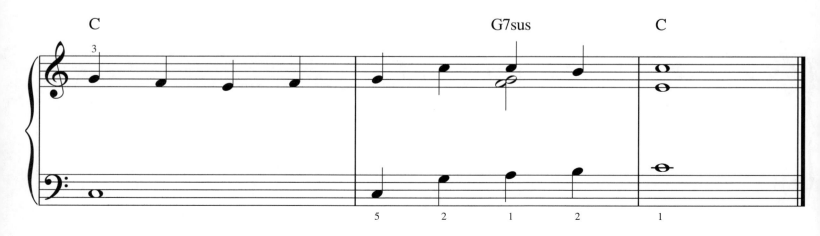

C   G7sus   C

(You Make Me Feel Like)
A NATURAL WOMAN

Words and Music by GERRY GOFFIN,
CAROLE KING and JERRY WEXLER

Moderate Swing Waltz tempo

Look-in' out on the morn-ing rain, _____
When my soul was in the lost and found, _____

I used to feel un - in -
you came a - long to

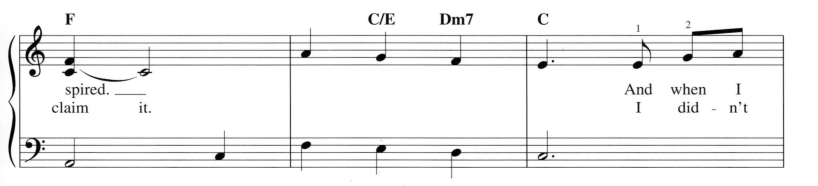

spired. _____
claim it.

And when I
I did - n't

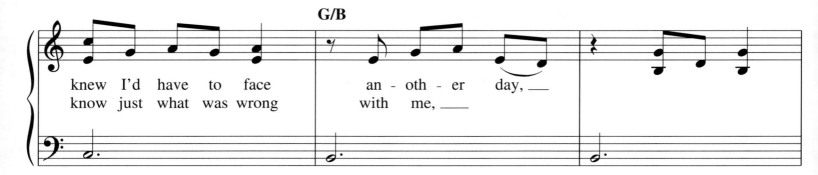

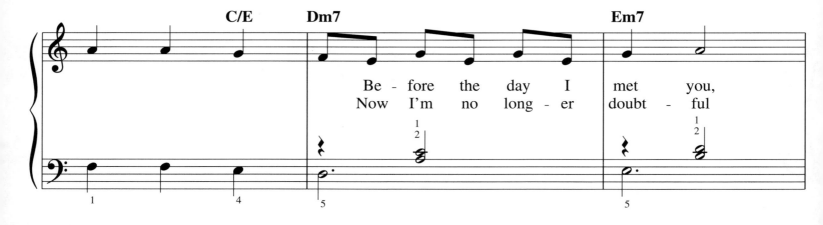

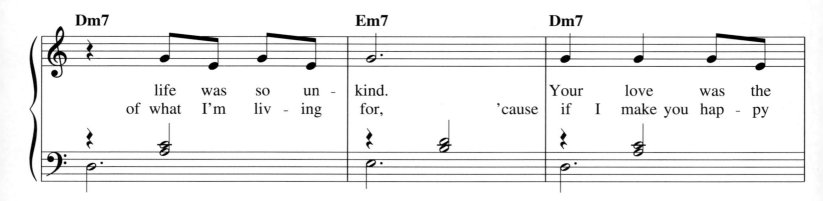

key to my ___ peace of mind, ___
I don't need to do ___ more, ___ } 'cause you make me ___

feel, _____   you make me ___ feel, _____

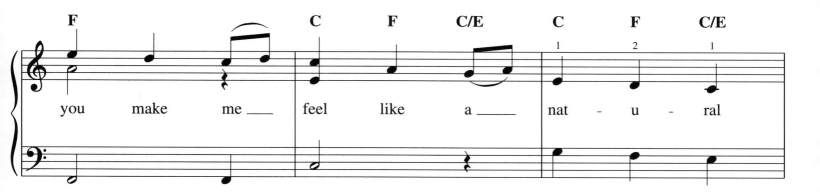

you make me ___ feel like a ___ nat - u - ral

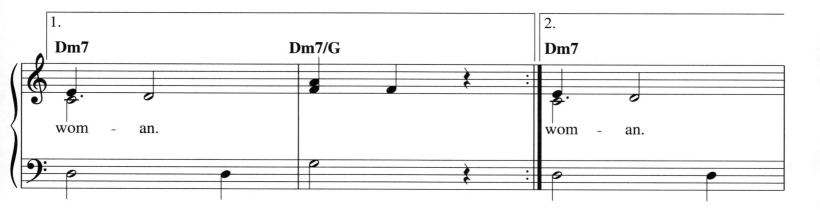

1.
wom - an.

2.
wom - an.

Oh, ___ ba - by, what you've

done to me! ___ (What you've done to me!) ___

You ___ make me feel ___ so ___ good in - side.

(Good in - side.) ___ And I just ___

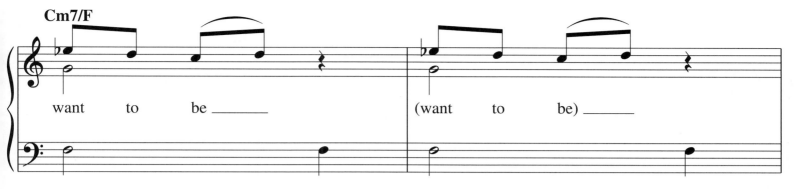

Cm7/F

want to be _____ (want to be) _____

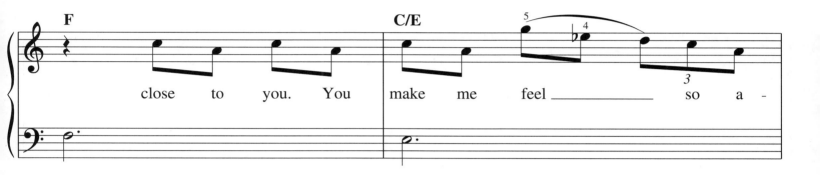

F   **C/E**

close to you. You make me feel _____ so a-

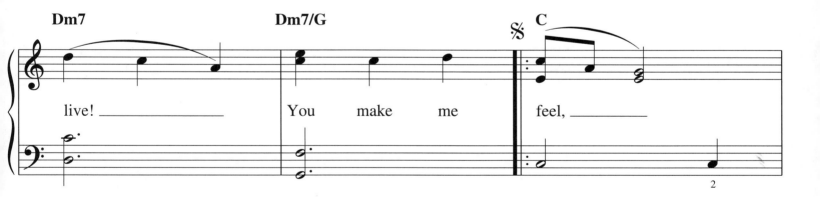

Dm7   **Dm7/G**   **C**

live! _____ You make me feel, _____

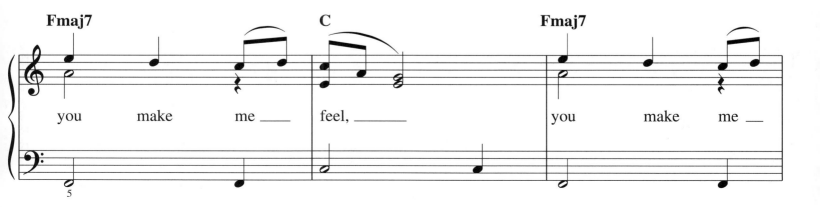

Fmaj7   **C**   **Fmaj7**

you make me _____ feel, _____ you make me _____

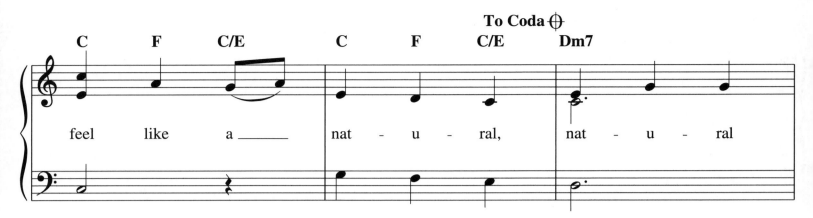

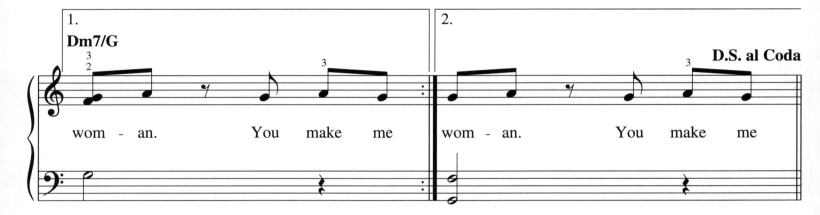

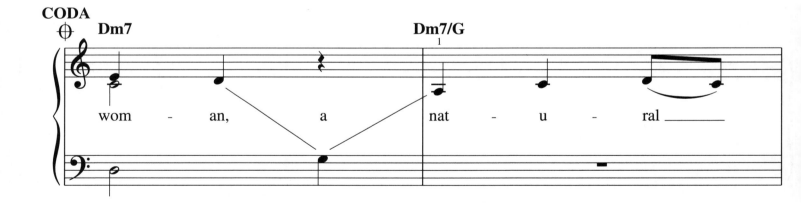

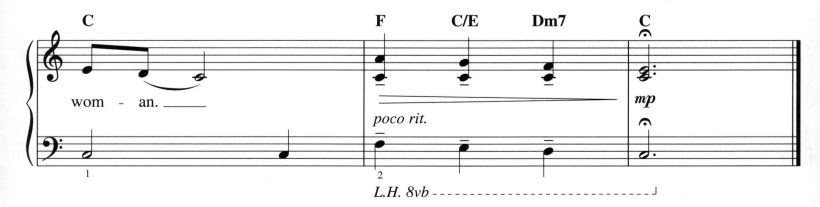